SEIKAI: CREST OF THE STARS:
Princess of the Empire

1
HIROYUKI MORIOKA

Seikai: Crest of the Stars 1
Princess of the Empire
Written by Hiroyuki Morioka

Translation - Sue Shambaugh
English Adaptation - Benjamin Arntz
Retouch and Lettering - Erika "skooter" Terriquez
Graphic Designer - Christian Lownds
Fan Consultants - Troy Christopher Haskin
Daniel Bonnell (ACIDSTEALTH)
Larry S. Moreland II
Editor - Kara Stambach
Senior Editor - Nicole Monastirsky
Digital Imaging Manager - Chris Buford
Pre-Production Supervisor - Lucas Rivera
Art Director - Anne Marie Horne
Production Manager - Elisabeth Brizzi
VP of Production - Ron Klamert
Editor in Chief - Rob Tokar
Publisher - Mike Kiley
President and C.O.O. - John Parker
C.E.O. and Chief Creative Officer - Stuart Levy

Crest designs by Tomas Montalvo-Lagos,
based on the original designs by Toshihiro Ono

A  Novel

TOKYOPOP Inc.
5900 Wilshire Blvd. Suite 2000
Los Angeles, CA 90036

E-mail: info@TOKYOPOP.com
Come visit us online at www.TOKYOPOP.com

ISBN: 1-59816-575-5

First TOKYOPOP printing: September 2006
10 9 8 7 6 5 4 3 2 1
Printed in the USA

Table of Contents

Characters:

Jinto	Son of Planet Martine's president
Lafiel	Pilot trainee on the patrol ship *Gosroth*
Bomowas Lexshu	Captain of the patrol ship *Gosroth*
Lowas Reilia	First Mate of the patrol ship *Gosroth*
Klowal	Governor of Baron Febdash Territory
Srguf	Klowal's father. Former Baron Febdash
Seelnay	Baron Febdash's vassal
Dorin	Jinto's friend from Planet Delktou

Letter From the Editor:

Dear *Seikai: Crest of the Stars* Fan:

Thank you so much for purchasing *Princess of the Empire*. I'm very proud to have been a part of bringing this long-anticipated novel to English-speaking audiences.

Morioka-sensei's epic space opera is a unique masterpiece. In the original Japanese version, all the text is in *kanji*, and then above those Japanese characters are the Abh language words (called Baronh) in *rubi* (a smaller, phonetic alphabet). Because of the way left-to-right English text is formatted for print, it was not possible for TOKYOPOP to put the entire book in English with foreign words in between the lines. So the decision was made to have most of the book in English, but to put phonetic Baronh in parentheses next to the English counterparts in narration, so that fans wouldn't miss out on the experience of Morioka-sensei's fantastic alien language. The only time Baronh is left untranslated is when it occurs in dialogue — this is to ensure the reader's suspension of disbelief, as no one speaks in parenthetical asides.

While working for several weeks with Fan Consultants from the Abh Nation to ensure a fair treatment of the Abh language, TOKYOPOP opted for a phonetic spelling of Abh words, rather than true, authentic Baronh (which has many silent letters and unusual spellings, confusing for a first-time reader not equipped with the Japanese-Baronh grammar guides available exclusively in Japan).

As you read, please check out the Glossary in the back of the book. I hope you enjoy getting familiar with all the different elements of language and culture that Morioka-sensei has created. If you are interested in learning more about Baronh in its complex form, please use the resources listed in the Notes and Glossary section.

I must thank Troy Christopher Haskin, Daniel Bonnell (aka ACIDSTEALTH), and Larry S. Moreland II, for all their passion and hard work.

Feedback is always welcome at the TOKYOPOP message boards! Please stay tuned for the second volume, *Seikai: Crest of the Stars: A Modest War*. And without further ado, enjoy *Princess of the Empire!*

Kara Allison Stambach
Junior Editor, Manga Novels

This crest depicts a Gaftonosh. The grotesque eight-headed dragon was long lost to the ages—forgotten, alive only in myth.

Resurrected on an Imperial crest, the Gaftonosh became infamous. The reason being that the empire which chose the dragon for its symbol became the strongest race in human history—creating an intergalactic civilization without parallel.

They were called the Abh, and they proudly referred to themselves as "kin of the stars."

At any rate, we'll restrict the story here to the Gaftonosh, because there are countless other books about the Abh.

—Excerpt from Monsters That Lived on Earth
by Roberto Lopez.

Prologue

Wow. Jinto Linn marveled at the night sky. *It's incredible.*

Like swarming bees, dozens of Abh battleships soared through the heavens, trailing long tails of light. Their incredible speed made them look shapeless, even when they flew disarmingly close to Planet Martine's surface. Floating menacingly amid the ships was a glowing orb that looked like the nucleus of an enormous atom.

Jinto watched the ominous sphere. He found its faint phosphorescence beautiful. The glowing ball was the remains of a manmade satellite that had mysteriously exploded thirty days earlier. Its slow orbit made the people of Martine anxious. Then one day, like a beehive awakening in the spring, Abh battleships began to materialize from the orb. This terrified the Martinese.

Although it was past his bedtime, Jinto now watched the luminous display from the rooftop garden of his residential complex. He was not supposed to be out so late alone; he was only eight years old. For old-timers intent on sticking to Earth's standard calendar, that actually worked out to ten years old. Either way, he was just a boy.

Long before Jinto was born, all of humanity dwelled in a star system they called the "Solar System," in honor of their sun. Intent on exploring the vastness of space, they launched innumerable spacecraft. On its maiden voyage, one research vessel named the *Oort Cloud* discovered a mysterious particle approximately three-tenths of a lightyear from the sun. It was only about a thousand times the mass of a proton, but somehow it radiated nearly five hundred megawatts of energy. No one on the *Oort Cloud* could determine the source of this energy.

The astronauts had hypotheses. One of them said there was a "white hole," and another said it was "null space" or "hyperspace." Regardless of the moniker, they all reasoned that mysterious particles of this nature were probably holes in the walls that separate one universe from another.

Scientists didn't get a chance to do much research on the nature and origin of these particles; they had barely named them Yuanons, when they were instructed to shift their research to focus on exploiting the particles' energy. (People were always on the lookout for potential sources of energy.)

At that time, mankind had developed nuclear fusion, which was mostly clean and efficient when used on Earth, but proved cumbersome in outer space. In order to reach a neighboring star, a nuclear-powered spacecraft had to be loaded with hundreds of times its own weight in fuel—that was an established fact of physics. This was not practical at all! Bussard-style Ramscoop propulsion was equally inefficient because of its relation to the density of interstellar matter. In short, every known fuel source simply weighed too much.

But if, and this was a *big* if, people could harness the power of the Yuanons, then they could throw all their previous methods of spacecraft propulsion right out the window. Fuel would be obsolete.

With many motivated minds concentrated on this task, it wasn't long before engineers drew up the specs for a Yuanon-powered spaceship. The ship was similar in shape to a giant tube, lined with superconductive materials that could absorb excess energy emitted by the Yuanons. Complicated magnets would then regulate the flow of this energy into the ship's propulsion systems, so that it could change directions. In theory, it was brilliant. In practical application, it was imperfect at best.

However, prescient that the population was growing at a rate the planet could not sustain, people had been exploring nearby star systems with unmanned probes for the purpose of colonization. Unfortunately, their research indicated that planets with atmospheric oxygen were extremely rare. Planets with oxygen, solar energy from a nearby star, and a gravitational pull similar to Earth's were even *more* rare. Planets like Earth were exceptions among exceptions; there really weren't many places for carbon-based life forms to live comfortably.

Although the Yuanon propulsion technology was not perfect, population growth necessitated interplanetary transit, and the demand for Yuanon-powered ships grew. So, with great effort, the first Yuanon propulsion spaceship was built, and aptly named the *Pioneer*. Capable of transporting equipment and people efficiently, the ship enabled humanity to commence with interstellar colonization.

Rather than use the ship to continue searching for needles in the endless haystack of space, people decided to make their own colonies; they devoted themselves to making teraforming technology — altering a planet's hostile conditions to make it suitable for human habitation.

Everyone was anxious to try this technology, so they went to the nearest planets that had even one characteristic in common with Earth. Mars and Venus were both relatively close and deemed adequate guinea pigs. Scientists increased the thin atmospheres to make breathing possible. They artificially simulated eons of erosion to create soil suitable for growing crops. Nascent technology enabled them to mass-produce water from scratch. They constructed entire artificial ecosystems.

These experiments on Mars and Venus were highly successful. As a bonus for the conscience of the human race, if they continued to make uninhabitable planets habitable, they'd never have to worry about pushing out any native species.

Once the new ecosystems were set up, ferries brought people to the artificial environments. As they expanded their living sphere, people found more and more Yuanons, which enabled them to build more and more ships. Whereas before, Yuanon ships were used exclusively for transporting materials, they now became integral to all aspects of the colonization process. This way, people could extend their reach far beyond the Solar System.

Engineers built a ship called the *Leif Erikson* that was only equipped for exploration and immigration — particularly the investigation and selection of potential residences. The government held a lottery to choose the *Leif Erikson's* crew. The ship was quickly stocked and launched with little ceremony.

Despite this bland sendoff, the passengers and crew of the *Leif Erikson* held high hopes. They weren't going to give up until they found a suitable planet. This determination was instrumental to their success.

Fully expecting to find an exotic ecosystem somewhere, the *Leif Erikson* drifted aimlessly through space for multiple generations, eventually finding a blue planet orbiting a G-type star. They named the star Hyde, after Martine Hyde, the ship's first captain, who never lived to see his dream fulfilled. In honor of his indomitable spirit, they called the blue planet Martine.

There was no intelligent life on Planet Martine, but peculiar flora and fauna abounded. The colonists, ever mindful of the strange ecosystem, increased their population slowly.

Having fulfilled its primary purpose, the interstellar immigration ship *Leif Erikson* remained in orbit around Planet Martine, almost like a monument satellite.

On the fifty-seventh day of the one hundred and second year after colonization, the *Leif Erikson* suddenly exploded without warning. All that remained of the vessel was a spherical, gaseous cloud, which continued to orbit the planet.

This nebulous cloud was actually comprised of the *Leif Erikson's* Yuanon, which had violently changed state and shape. Because it phosphoresced such brilliant colors, people eventually regarded it fondly, as if it were Martine's moon.

Unexpectedly, a spaceship materialized from within the gaseous lump and immediately circled Planet Martine. The ship refused all requests for communication, increasing the anxiety of Martine's inhabitants. After its third circuit around Martine, the ship vanished as quickly as it came, disappearing into the faintly glowing sphere of the Yuanon cloud.

Twenty-four days later, on the eighty-first day of the year, an entire flying armada emerged from the spherical space.

Identifying themselves as the Abh, the people inside the ships wanted to communicate this time. Conversation was possible because the recon ship that came three weeks earlier determined that the Martine language was based on English. The Abh had high-tech machines that instantly translated their own guttural language into perfectly articulated English.

When the Abh appeared on the Martinese video-conferencing screens, they were all young and beautiful, incredibly similar in appearance to humans, except for their electric-blue hair. "Despite some physical differences, we are also children of Earth," the Abh explained. "We've simply adjusted our genes slightly."

The Abh said they ruled approximately fifteen hundred inhabited star systems and more than twenty thousand partially inhabited star systems. Their massive territory reached such vast corners of the universe that it was called Humankind Empire of Abh (Frybar Gloer Gor Bari), or simply "Abh Empire" (Frybar) for short.

Ever optimistic, the Martine government requested friendly negotiations. Commander-in-Chief Abriel, the leader of the Abh invasion fleet, flatly refused.

"Regrettably," Abriel said with no hint of actual regret, "we cannot do that. Our mission is not to make friends for the Empire, but to add new worlds to Her Majesty the Empress' territory."

Because the Abh sent a heavily armed battle fleet rather than an unarmed ship, the people of Martine were not terribly surprised to hear the Abh's objective. They were surprised, however, by the candor with which Abriel announced these intentions.

The people of Martine wanted to appeal to a diplomat — surely there had to be someone with more authority who would be sympathetic to their plight.

"I am not just a soldier," Abriel explained. "I am also a diplomat."

But of what rank? With what authority? The people of Martine wanted to know.

"Actually, I am the crown prince. My will is the will of the Empire." He paused. "I understand your anxiety, but I will not enter negotiations concerning your independence. I will, however, clarify your position as subjects of the Empire."

After a brief deliberation, the government concluded that, since the invasion would affect the entire population of the planet, the Abh's address should be broadcast. So, the government relayed the image of the commander-in-chief speaking from the flagship to the video screens for the general public, giving the citizens their first look at the invader.

Most people thought he looked like an elf. Pointed ears poked out of Abriel's waist-long hair, which was the color of a blue raspberry frozen yogurt. His pallid face suggested an approximate age of twenty-five. His features were so delicate, his expression so languid, he could have easily been mistaken for a woman who found the subjugation of star systems to be quite tedious.

"Now. I will relate the gist of the relationship between the Empire and land worlds," the crown prince of the Abh Empire began calmly. "Due to this star system's special characteristics, Her Majesty the Empress will be your ruler, at least for the time being. Since she is enormously busy, she will dispatch a noble representative or a Fapyut . . . that means Sovereign.

"In general, we do not enjoy the unsophisticated triviality of governing land worlds; as long as your surface dwellers can maintain order, our representative will not be obtrusive to your daily operations.

"You will also need to select an official to serve as a negotiator with the sovereign and the central Empire. You may call your official whatever you like: President, Chief, Chairman, Kaiser, even Emperor if it comforts you to maintain the illusion that you are an independent nation. Our documents will refer to this official as the Territorial Representative.

"How you choose this official is entirely up to you. Election, heredity, or lottery—it is of no importance to us. However, we do exercise final approval of any appointed official. This is mostly a formality, but we won't allow one who advocates secession from the Empire.

"The sovereign does not have the right to tax you. But the Empire retains the right to monopolize commerce with other star systems. All profits from your interstellar trade will go to the funding of Imperial activities. Depending on the economic potential, we may opt to invest in your planet or other planets in your star system. And, in order to protect our investment, it may be necessary for us to implement a garrison that will operate independently from your governmental mechanism.

"The Empire will impose two conditions on you. One, we prohibit the construction of spaceships capable of interstellar travel. Although Imperial technology enables us to fly faster than the speed of light, do not even consider this for your people.

"Also, you are not to attempt traveling to other star systems through normal space. We simply will not allow it; we must preserve our monopoly on interstellar business. With the sovereign's approval, however, you may own spaceships for travel within your star system. But under no circumstances may these ships be armed.

"Our second demand is the construction of a recruitment office for the Imperial Star Force. We will dispatch officers whose authority will be limited to issues of your defense. Based on your population, this shouldn't equate to more than a hundred persons. As long as your autonomous government functions properly, we will not deploy more officers without your consent. Neither will we conscript soldiers; participation in our Star Force is entirely voluntary. Keep in mind, though, we will not tolerate activities that hinder anyone's decision to volunteer.

"Your people will be known as territorial citizens, but volunteer members of the Star Force become vassals of the sovereign. This means that if you choose to work for the Empire, you will become an Imperial citizen and fall under the umbrella of the Empire's protection.

"Your everyday lives may change dramatically, but not from Imperial imposition; rather, the imports our interstellar trade brings to your planet will cause these changes. Once you become accustomed to the new goods, most of you territorial citizens will be able to function normally, only subconsciously aware that you are subjects of the Empire.

"This concludes my statement.

"Doubtless, you have countless questions for my subordinates. Please decide whether you will accept these conditions peacefully, or if you wish us to force them on you. Although your planet contains many valuable resources, I will not hesitate to decimate as much of it as it takes to make you submit.

"Luckily for us, your capital city is very contained; we can likely destroy it without damaging the valuable surrounding environment.

"Now, feel free to pester my underlings with your questions, but know that there are limits to their patience. You have exactly three planetary rotations from now to respond. Transmission complete."

The people of Martine did not care for Abh manners.

Although Abriel's tone was courteous, he made no attempts to disguise his extreme indifference to their existence. Martine's governmental officials found Abriel's arrogance particularly infuriating. Was it really necessary for him to label their jobs—jobs they'd worked extremely hard to attain—as "unsophisticated trivialities"?

Although Abriel stated that Imperial subjects were granted a high level of autonomy, the Martinese were not certain whether to believe him. Perhaps, in truth, the Empire was cruel and despotic.

Frustrated, the bureaucrats pelted the Abh officers with innumerable questions. The responses they received were ambiguous; it was impossible to determine the Abh's level of trustworthiness. Short on time, the governmental representatives called for backup: Martine's best lawyers. The attorneys grilled the invaders, but were unable to unearth any misstatements or contradictions.

As Martine's citizens came to their planet from elsewhere in space, they'd predicted that other colonizers would also appear someday. Fearing potential hostility, they'd even built an anti-invasion defense system.

Unfortunately, this defense system was not a top priority in the budget. There were fewer than ten anti-invasion lasers, and only about twenty anti-spacecraft missiles. There was no Martinese Space Army—there wasn't even an office. Instead, there was a small room behind the janitorial closet where the laser and missile maintenance records collected dust. During a crisis, control of the weapons fell to one semi-retired general, who often slept in the underground control room because it made him feel important.

The only other institution even remotely resembling a military force on Martine was its police force, which was equipped to handle a large-scale riot of unarmed civilians, but not a fleet of heavily armed spacecraft.

Regardless, a faction of Congress called for resistance, reasoning that the large space fleet was probably just a bluff. And, although outmatched in space, if they could somehow bring the battle down to the surface, they could certainly beat the Abh. The pillar of their argument was honor; how could they surrender without even fighting?

Those opposed to war were equally obdurate, and arguments ensued. Heads butted, philosophies clashed, and pigheaded men slandered each other. This only set the opposing sides deeper into the trenches of their respective mindsets. Even though a Martine day was two hours longer than an Earth day, they only had three of them to make up their minds. That wasn't very much time at all.

Frustrated, Congress did manage to agree that they were never going to come to an agreement. Ultimately, they left the decision to the president.

Rock Linn, Jinto's father, was the president.

President Linn made an executive decision and ran it by his trusted advisors, who issued him their wholehearted support. Of course, his decision could not possibly please everyone.

As the deadline drew near, President Linn stood before the presidential mansion's communication equipment, prepared to give his answer.

Elsewhere, Jinto stared at the lightshow in the sky, completely engrossed. He'd never seen anything so beautiful or frightening in his life.

"I've been looking for you."

Jinto turned around to see Teal Clint, his father's private secretary. A tall, thin man, Teal Clint had worked for President Linn since the latter had been a mere congressman—before Jinto was even born.

Before Jinto could utter his first words, his mother, a mining supervisor, died in a freak accident. Rock Linn, ill-prepared to deal with a son as a single father, asked Teal and his wife, Lena, to raise Jinto. The Clints had no children of their own, and gladly accepted.

Until he went to school and overheard classroom gossip, Jinto actually believed he was Teal's son. He continued to love the chief secretary like a father, even after the discovery that Rock Linn was his biological parent. As for Lena Clint, he loved her more than anyone else in the world.

There, on the rooftop garden, a shadow hung over Teal's already swarthy face.

"I'm sorry," Jinto apologized, thinking he might be scolded for staying outside so late, especially on such a dangerous night. "I'll go back to my room right away."

"It's okay. Come with me," Teal commanded.

"Where are we going?" Jinto asked, somewhat frightened by Teal's grave tone.

"The presidental mansion."

"The mansion? Why are we going there?"

"Just come with me," Teal demanded, turning to go.

Grandon City was Planet Martine's only metropolis. Within its walls, there were three residential complexes, sensibly named Omni I, Omni II, and Omni III. The Clints lived in Omni III, but the president's mansion was all the way over in Omni I. For Jinto, a trip to the presidential mansion invariably meant seeing his father. *What could Father possibly want with me at a time like this? And doesn't Teal Clint, the president's chief secretary, have something more important to do than fetch an eight-year-old?*

"Hey, wait," Jinto called, unable to keep up with Teal's long strides. Teal was usually considerate of the differences in height, and normally accommodated Jinto by walking slower. *Why is there such a rush tonight?*

"Time is short. Hurry," Teal said without slowing his pace.

Jinto managed to catch up to Teal in front of the elevator. "Are you mad at me? Whatever I did . . ."

Teal did not respond, but impatiently mashed the elevator call button a few times. Jinto started to get really nervous. When the elevator door opened and no one else was inside, Jinto wasn't a hundred percent sure he wanted to go. He didn't have time to think it over much, as Teal quickly ushered him into the elevator.

"Nexus Floor," Teal instructed the elevator's voice-activated control system.

The door closed and they began the descent in silence.

"You think we can win?" Jinto asked when he couldn't take the silence anymore.

"It's not about winning or losing; it's not a war." Teal sounded disgusted.

"We surrendered?"

Teal glared. "Yes. Your father waved the white flag. He sold us out."

"What do you mean?"

"That bastard made a deal. A filthy deal," Teal spat out viciously.

"Deal?"

"What are you, a parrot?"

"S-sorry," Jinto apologized, hanging his head.

Teal sighed. "I didn't want a war either. There's no way we could win. But to make a deal like that . . ." he paused. "Damn it! I really misjudged that asshole!"

Secretly proud to have two fathers, it pained Jinto to see the one who raised him badmouthing his sire.

When Jinto's eyes started to water, and Teal could see sadness twist the boy's face, the older man instantly felt guilty. "Sorry. It's not your fault."

"What happened, anyway?"

"Oh, right," Teal said, tousling Jinto's short, black hair. "Like I said, Rock made a deal. He's going to announce the details in about ten minutes. After that, everyone on this planet is going to hate him. They will hate him enough to hate you, just because you're his son. That's why we're going to the presidential mansion—it's more secure."

"Are they going to kill me?" Jinto shuddered.

"Don't know. They might try. At the very least, they will hate you—they will curse your name and throw things at you. I wouldn't be surprised if someone threw a smoke bomb into your room."

"What about Lena?" Jinto asked automatically. "A lot of people know I live with you."

"I already contacted her. Besides, Lena's an adult. She can take care of herself."

"So she already left?" Jinto asked, surprised she would go without him.

"Yes," Teal said, "but she was extremely worried about you. She made me promise to find you."

"Oh. I see." Jinto felt relieved that she had thought of him. Now it was his turn to be worried for her—since there was no guarantee that Teal would find him, who's to say Lena wouldn't conduct her own search?

The elevator arrived at the Nexus Floor and the door opened. Silently, they exited. Countless elevator tubes lined the Nexus Floor in a design somewhat reminiscent of an ancient temple's columns. In addition to the vertical elevators, the floor was inundated with taxi boxes, which were essentially laterally moving elevators. The taxi boxes were programmed to arrive right in front of the elevator doors.

Teal motioned Jinto into a waiting taxi box. Jinto sat still, but his heart continued to race.

"The president's mansion. No stops." Teal ordered the taxi box. Once again, he fell silent.

Extremely intimidated but infinitely curious, Jinto wondered what kind of "deal" his father had made. *This isn't really the right time to ask. But if not now, when?* "What is the deal, Teal?"

"It's classified. We can't let the general public know about it until the announcement."

"Even me?"

Teal scoffed. "Are you pulling rank already? You little stinker."

Jinto smiled.

"Put on the holo. The announcement will come on soon."

Always quick to follow orders, Jinto pushed the taxi box's holovision switch. Immediately, a hologram appeared where the taxi box's manual controls were. The hologram was of a man—a miniature, translucent newscaster—broadcasting live updates.

"Now, a breaking report," the tiny, semitransparent man said. "At this time, we're receiving reports that the Abh ships aren't leaving. Sources close to President Linn speculate the president plans to surrender to the Empire. I, for one, sincerely hope this is just speculation. Oh. I'm receiving another report—the president is going to make an announcement at exactly twenty-five hundred hours. That's in one minute and thirty seconds."

The newscaster did his best to fill the longest ninety seconds of Jinto's life. But Jinto was too anxious for the announcement and too scared of its contents to pay attention to the holovision. Instead, he watched Teal, who stared straight ahead, as still as a statue.

The taxi box exited the complex, rocketing through the liaison tube that served as a vehicular bridge over the jungle.

Finally, it was time.

The image of the newsman cut to a traditional press conference room with an unmanned podium. A solemn spokesperson stepped up to the mike.

"As you may have already heard, I have an announcement."

Jinto held his breath.

"Today, at 23:52, President Rock Linn handed over control of the Hyde star system to His Highness Dusanyu, Crown Prince, and Imperial Fleet Commander-in-Chief King Abriel Nei Lamsar Balkei. From this day forth, Planet Martine is part of the Abh Empire of Humankind."

Although the press weren't visible in the hologram, their resignation was certainly audible. They weren't surprised or angry, just disappointed. "Just as I expected," said one of the faceless reporters.

That isn't so bad, Jinto thought, scanning Teal's face for any hint of a reaction.

Seeing Jinto's confusion, Teal spoke up. "There's more," he explained stoically.

"President Linn," continued the spokesman, "proposed a compromise."

"Can he do that?" asked someone from the media.

"Try to bear with me for a minute; I'll take questions at the end. In exchange for the override codes to our anti-spacecraft weapons, he requested that the new sovereign be a citizen of the Hyde star system."

"And did the Abh accept?"

"Please be seated and save your questions for the end, okay? Thank you. Apparently, the Abh were more apprehensive of our weaponry than we thought; they accepted the president's terms."

"Who will our Fapyut be?"

The spokesman sighed. "As Commander-in-Chief Abriel explained, the sovereign is more like the owner of a space trading company than a governmental figure. As you all know, the owners of most businesses are chosen by heredity, not democracy."

"Bull!" The disembodied voices were getting discernibly more agitated. "You better tell us it's not who we think it is!"

"This can't be happening," Jinto said to himself.

Teal kept his mouth shut.

Exasperated, the spokesperson sighed. "I see there's no fooling you; the new sovereign to the star system will be Rock Linn."

The ethereal voices were undeniably pissed.

"Now you get it?" Teal asked. "He gave away our independence and the only weapon we had, just to become a nobleman. I never thought they'd take that deal. They must have been more afraid of our weapons than we thought. Who knows? Maybe we could have won!"

"But, but . . ." Jinto trailed off, trying to defend his father's honor. "Maybe my father requested an election."

"There's no way of knowing." Teal ground his teeth. "We only heard the terms of the agreement after it was done . . . after the Abh deactivated our defense system . . . after the Linn family became Imperial nobles. The bastard never even consulted me. Me, *Chief Secretary!* I thought I was his friend, his confidant. Turns out he just needed me to take care of his kid."

So that's it! Jinto thought. *Teal's taking it personally.*

After many futile attempts, the hologram spokesperson finally gained order, yelling, "For goodness' sake, behave yourselves!" Satisfied with the results, he continued. "If you think it through, you'll see this is really the best possible solution. Sovereign Linn will be more sympathetic to our needs than an imported ruler. He is committed to following our established democratic rules, as long as we don't violate any of the Empire's laws. Here's a question for *you*. Could we expect that from a native Imperial noble? I don't think so. We will retain the largest degree of autonomy of any star system in the Empire."

"Poppycock!"

"Why should we trust Linn?"

"Yeah, why isn't he here, making this announcement himself?"

"Where is he? Where's President—I mean Sovereign—Linn?"

Noticeably flustered, the spokesperson was reluctant to speak. "In order to finalize the details of the agreement, Rock Linn has gone to the Imperial capital, Lakfakalle. He boarded an Abh landing craft on French Plain. Right now, he's probably already aboard the fleet's flagship."

"The jackass ran away!" someone yelled.

"Is he coming back?" another asked.

"Oh, he'll come back—with a boatload of Imperial bodyguards!"

"The Empire won't make him a nobleman. They're lying to him, and it serves him right!"

"Everyone, please!" The spokesperson frantically tried to calm them down. "Please understand, the motivation behind the president's decision is our collective well-being, not his own, so—" Jinto flipped the holovision off.

"There it is," Teal said. "After Rock, you'll be the next sovereign. You're our prince now, Jinto. Whoops. Please forgive me any rudeness, Your Highness. Excuse me. Excuse me."

Teal bowed excessively to augment his bitter jibe.

"That's not fair, Teal." Jinto was on the verge of tears.

"I know." Teal still couldn't look at the boy. "I know I shouldn't take it out on you, but damn it! I don't even know what to think right now."

The taxi box entered the Nexus Floor of Omni I. It wouldn't be long until they reached the elevator to the presidential mansion.

"Tell me one thing, Teal."

"What's that?"

"When you told Lena to run away . . ." Jinto didn't want to finish the question, but he was just too curious. "Did you tell her about the deal, too?"

Teal hesitated just long enough to make the truth of his answer suspect. "No. It was classified."

"I see." Jinto could practically hear the sound of his beloved, familiar world falling to pieces.

1 Delktou Spaceport (Bidaut Delktour)

It's different from how I remember it.

Noise assaulted Jinto as he emerged from the surface-to-spaceport Dobroria. He paused before the ascent-tube.

Oh well. At least the gravity is the same as on Delktou, so I won't puke.

Jinto tried to recall the details of his only previous trip to the spaceport. That was seven years before, when he came to Planet Delktou from Planet Martine, or Martinu, as the Abh called it.

I must have passed through here on my way to the Rebisath's stateroom, he thought. The memory of the passenger ship was hazy, at best.

With all sorts of ascent-tubes sprouting out of the huge, circular floor, the spaceport reminded Jinto of the Nexus Floor of the complex where he grew up. There was one glaring difference, however; the spaceport boasted a huge banquet hall.

Lined with tables and chairs, the hall was full of jovial people speaking languages from all corners of the universe. Both human waiters and robotic vending machines hustled from table to table, serving food and drinks.

The people of Delktou sure know how to kill time, Jinto thought. *I wonder if it'll be like this in Frybar spaceports.* `

Periodically, the informational announcements overpowered the background music. "Will passengers booked on the ship *Lengarf Glorn* to Estote Park at 17:30 please report to Dobroria Seventeen to finalize boarding procedures."

The informational broadcasts always came over the loudspeaker twice; first in Delktou's native tongue, then in the Abh language.

A few disgruntled passengers exited the banquet hall, pushing past Jinto and his rolling suitcase. As they exited, the noise of the spaceport swallowed them up.

"To all passengers disembarking from the ship *Sellef Nizeil*, thank you for your patience, and welcome to Dreujhe Vorlak! An expedited surface-bound descent-tube will depart in three minutes."

A group of passengers, who appeared to have recently gotten off the *Sellef Nizeil*, made no moves toward the descent tubes. They were too busy consuming massive quantities of liquor (Skiade) in what looked like a spirited drinking contest.

How many drunk people miss their ships every day? Jinto wondered.

It was a valid quality; most passengers leaving the star system were immigrants, for whom this would be a once-in-a-lifetime space voyage. So of course they wanted to make the most of it.

No one invited Jinto for a drink. He didn't expect them to—although Delktou's people were generally friendly, no one had spoken to Jinto since he first got into the ascent-tube. When he approached people, they looked the other way. He felt extremely isolated.

Wearing the standard-issue garments for an Imperial noble (addressed as Rue Sif), Jinto realized how ridiculous he must have looked. *People would have to be nuts to talk to someone like me.*

There was nothing wrong with Jinto's bodysuit (Sorf); it was very modern. The problem was the long robe (called a Daush), he wore on top of it. A shoulder-to-foot garment, the robe billowed, except where Jinto's sash (Kutaroev) cinched it around his waist. On top of that, the thing was sleeveless, with stiff shoulder pads that looked like upside-down triangles. The cuffs and collar had a thick, scarlet border.

The computer crystal (a Datykirl) built into Jinto's wristband computer (Kreuno) was green, to prove his family's status as rising noblity. Though he didn't know it, the elegant crown (known as an Alpha) on his head also corresponded to Jinto's social status, since he was pretty much guaranteed the right to wear the Imperial Crest Medal (Gal Skas).

This was the first day that Jinto had dressed as a noble. The result was only slightly less foolish-looking than he'd anticipated. His shoulders were a bit wider than those of a typical Abh, but everything was probably within the acceptable range.

However, Jinto was clearly not an Abh; his light brown hair gave him away. On top of that, it was common for Imperial nobles to be left alone in an Imperial spaceport.

"Hey! Linn Jinto!"

At first, Jinto thought he was hearing things. But on Delktou, unlike Martine, they use the family name first, so that was definitely his name. Maybe he'd misheard, or maybe somebody else had the same name.

Jinto smiled when he spotted a beefy boy occupying a four-person table.

"Ku Dorin!" Jinto called, half running to the table. "What are you doing here?"

"I came to see you off, knucklehead!"

"Gee, thanks," Jinto laughed.

"I'm sorry. Is Your Nobleness offended by the presence of a poor commoner kid?"

Jinto smiled. "Don't you know what 'thanks' means?"

"Oh. Is *that* what you said? Your imitation immigrant accent is so thick! Sit down already. I'm tired of waiting."

"I wish you'd called. We could have met properly." Jinto sat and looked around expectantly.

Dorin squirmed. "The others aren't coming. I'm the only one who's seeing you off."

"I see," Jinto said, trying unsuccessfully to hide his disappointment.

"To tell you the truth, I was nervous about it, too. I thought you might ignore me."

"What? Why?" Jinto frowned. "Come on. We're bound by the sport of minchiu! I could never ignore you."

A cross between soccer and roller derby, minchiu was the most popular sport in Delktou society. Teams comprised ten members. Delktou had a professional minchiu league, and every region, school, corporation, and hospital seemed to have a team.

At his school, Jinto had discovered an aptitude for the game. He joined a regional team. There, he'd made his first friends, starting with Ku Dorin.

However, Jinto kept one secret from the minchiu team; he pretended to be the child of ordinary immigrants. He'd only confessed his status as Rue Sif three days earlier, when he told his teammates that he had to leave Delktou. The air couldn't have been chillier if he'd confessed to murder. It was so unbearable, Jinto literally ran away from the scene.

"Who knew how you'd act? Who really knew anything about you?" As soon as he said it, Dorin's face turned dark.

"Fair enough," Jinto said. "Maybe it's my fault for keeping it a secret. But, tell me this—if I'd said I was a noble, you think they would have accepted me?"

Dorin shook his head. "No, probably not."

"Definitely not."

"Nobody knew how to behave around a noble. I mean, we've never even seen a *Lef*," Dorin said, wrinkling his nose at the Abh word for gentry.

"I get it. I don't even know how to behave, myself."

"Deep," Dorin assessed. "You know, those Sif clothes really suit you."

"This clown suit?" Jinto pinched the Daush in his fingers. "Come on. I know how ridiculously un-Abh I look."

"No, no. You don't stand out at all."

Jinto grinned. "Stop that."

"Are you on your way home from here?"

"What?" Jinto realized he'd forgotten to tell anyone where he was going. "Oh! No. I'm going to Lakfakalle."

"The Imperial capital? The Arosh?"

"Yeah, studying abroad again. Kenru Sazoir this time."

"What's that?" Dorin asked. It certainly *sounded* impressive.

"A school that specializes in training military administrators," Jinto explained. "It's an officer school. The Abh call it Lodairl Sazoir. I took the exam two months ago at Labule's Banzorl Ludorlt."

Dorin's eyes popped open. "So you're joining the Star Force?"

"Yeah."

"But you have a Ribeun. Why bother?"

"I've got a territory, but there's more to inheriting a Sune than being born into a noble family. To earn my title,

I'm actually required to serve as an officer—who are called Lodair—for at least ten years. The only reason my father didn't have to do it was because he was already middle-aged at the time of his appointment."

"Sounds hard, being a Sif."

"Yeah. It's depressing; three years as a Kenyu in the Star Force, ten years as an officer—that's thirteen years of military life. On the other hand, I guess it makes sense that the Frybar requires military service proportional to your social station."

"Will you ever go home?"

"Eventually, I'll have to. It's my Ribeun." Jinto felt odd, calling his old home his territory.

"I meant now. You've already been gone a long time," Dorin said, trying to imagine what it would be like to leave Delktou for so long.

"Yeah, well . . ." Although he received monthly news updates from his father, Jinto hadn't set foot on Martine in seven years—long enough to doubt his ability to speak Martinese properly. The last news Jinto heard from his father was that Teal Clint was the leader of a volatile group of anti-Empire insurgents.

"It doesn't seem like *my* home, anyway. All the people there hate me."

"Huh." Dorin didn't understand Jinto's indifference to his home planet. The people of Delktou loved their planet and feared leaving more than anything else. "But you still want to be the sovereign?"

"No, I don't," Jinto spoke at the table. "But even if I renounced my inheritance and went back to being a regular citizen of Martine, I'd never be forgiven. The best I could ever do is become a citizen of Delktou."

"So why don't you do that?" Dorin demanded indignantly.

"I'm not sure I can redeem myself in the eyes of the people, but my father seems to think I can."

"And you believe him?"

"He's very persuasive. I'm convinced he's working for the sake of the Hyde star system, and I intend to do that too, if I can."

Rock Linn had given his son an earful on the subject. Martine had immense resources, he explained, just like Earth. The planet already had a glut of incredible fauna, which had only increased through Martinese gene-splicing experiments.

If the Martinese could trade their bioresources with other star systems, then they would become enormously wealthy. And if they entrusted this trade to the Rue Sif, it would be much easier for the profits to spill over into the hands of the general public. Thus, everyone won.

In order to ensure the proper allocation of the proceeds, a citizen of the Hyde star system had to be its ruler and govern the trade.

"Ah, I can understand that," Dorin said after Jinto finished his explanation.

"That's why I'm still a noble. But there's one problem with the whole scheme."

"What's that?"

"Well, I'm not a citizen of the Hyde star system anymore; it's impossible to be a citizen of Hyde star system *and* an Abh noble simultaneously. We have no Hyde citizenship rights. My children will be engineered, both genetically and culturally; beautiful, blue-haired Abh—in body and spirit. So who's to say how many generations of the Linn family will continue to work for the good of the Hyde people?"

Dorin looked impressed. "You're too serious, man. Forget about all the people who hate you and start thinking about yourself. Decide whether or not you actually *want* to fill your father's shoes. Personally, I wouldn't want to forfeit such a huge business, but maybe that's just me."

Fill my father's shoes, huh? Jinto pondered, amused. If he didn't become the next count (Dreu), the Linn family legacy would come to an end. *And so what? Who would really care?*

"You're right," Jinto acquiesced.

"Of course I'm right," Dorin stated. He suddenly pointed at the floor. "You know, this is the first time I've ever been up in the spaceport. From up here, Delktou looks really awesome."

"Yes," Jinto agreed. "It does."

Underneath the table was a video screen displaying an aerial view of the planet. From their position, the orbital tower (called an Arnej) connecting the surface to the spaceport looked small and weak, as if made of dental floss. Shrouded in clouds, the planet disappeared in the light from the star named Vorash. Jinto suddenly realized he'd never looked down on his true home planet.

"How long have you been here again? Five years?" Dorin asked.

"Seven," Jinto said, snapping out of his trance. "The invasion of the Hyde star system was in the year Ruecoth 945."

"Wow. And they hustled you out of there right away?"

"Yeah. Like an animal being taken to the zoo, they threw me into a departing Frash, then took me to an orbiting Rebisath before I even knew what was happening."

"You must have had an attendant, right?" Dorin asked as he scrounged up some coins and put them into a passing vending machine. He selected two coffees (Surgu). He offered one to Jinto. "Here, my treat."

"Thanks."

"No problem. It's not everyday you get to treat the son of a Voda."

Jinto smiled. "After I left Martine, I never had an attendant."

"But you were only . . ." Dorin trailed off, thwarted by numbers again. "What, eleven?"

"Ten."

"What kind of nincompoop sends a ten-year-old kid to another star system all by himself?"

"Well, I wasn't entirely alone. They assigned one of the Rebisath's duty clerks to me, probably at my father's request. She helped me out—brought me meals and stuff."

"That's sweet. Luxurious," Dorin said enviously. "An elegant space journey."

"It wasn't like that. Really," Jinto pleaded, sipping his Surgu. "I couldn't even speak to her. At the time, there wasn't a mechanical interpreter that could speak Martinese. She tried to do something with a machine fluent in ancient English, but—"

"What's English?"

"Martinese is derived from ancient English, which traces all the way back to Earth. But it's very different from Martinese, and I never learned it, so it's gibberish to me."

"Just like Abh!" Like most Delktou people, Dorin knew no Abh.

"Yes. But it didn't matter. I didn't feel like talking to her anyway."

"Was she Abh?"

"It didn't matter. At the time, she was just 'one of the invaders.' I remember she had black hair, so in hindsight, she was definitely born on a land world. Probably a Rue Lef."

"If she were Abh, maybe you would have liked her more," Dorin suggested.

"What makes you say that?"

"Jeez, man, they're all gorgeous!"

Jinto took slight offense. "She was really nice to me at a time when I had no one else. She got me through all the enrollment procedures here. And despite all her help, I never even learned her name. She probably told me, but I couldn't separate it from the gibberish."

"What a story! Sounds like the first chapter to an epic romance. Too bad she's probably old enough to be your grandma now. If she were Abh though, you wouldn't know it."

Abh people didn't age.

Jinto just shook his head. *He's so incorrigible.*

"What?" Dorin asked, hoping to placate Jinto. "You know I've got ladies on the brain twenty-seven hours a day."

Undeniably true, Jinto thought. "You always blow every relationship out of proportion. I mean, if you sideswiped someone in traffic, you'd call her your girlfriend."

"I'm offended. I am," Dorin announced with feigned umbrage. "I mean, for starters, she'd have to be cute. Really, really cute. Second, I don't want a girlfriend. One night's enough."

"Hah!" Jinto slapped his knee. "How would you know?"

"Personal experience."

"No way! You've never been with a woman!"

Dorin used two fingers to direct Jinto's eyes to his. Very deliberately, he said, "Seriously."

"Yeah, right! I've only ever seen you with a girl once, and I think she was your sister."

"Look, you said never. Compared to never, once is as big as infinity."

"Gross! That's your sister we're talking about! I didn't know you were into that sort of thing."

"Shut up. I'm not talking about my sister. I've hooked up with someone who isn't related to me."

"Just once?"

"So many times, I can't count!" Dorin said indignantly. "You just never met her."

"Oh."

"And what about you?" Dorin asked. "You're so repressed. It's not healthy. You need to get out there and find a woman. Unless," Dorin smiled coyly, "you're not into *that* sort of thing."

Jinto played along. "You got me. But don't worry. No matter how much it pains me, I won't put the moves on you."

"It's never too late, Jinto. Just say the word, and I'm yours."

"With all these people watching?"

"Who are they to judge our love?"

Jinto laughed. "You should be careful, talking like that—if I weren't straight, I might have gone for it."

Dorin laughed. "Don't worry—I wouldn't let it get out of hand. If you're straight, then I'm fanatically hetero. But only because I wouldn't have any guy except you."

"True. Cheers," Jinto toasted. They polished off the coffee and threw the paper cups into the trash receptacle in the table's center. "Thanks."

"The least I can do for a young noble," Dorin said smugly, glancing to the right. He nudged Jinto. "Check it out."

Jinto turned and looked.

At the next table sat a dark, middle-aged woman, her brown eyes rudely surveying Jinto's Sif garments and brown hair.

What would I do, Jinto thought, *if I were a real Abh nobleman? Shout at her for being rude? Ignore her? Or would I shoot her dead with no explanation?*

Dissatisfied with these choices, Jinto simply chose to flash her a smarmy smile.

Busted, the middle-aged woman averted her gaze.

Jinto sighed.

"Look at you! That old broad is totally hot for you. If I could just borrow your face for a while . . ."

"It's the clothes," Jinto explained. "A lander wearing Imperial clothes is as common as a dog using Grei to eat."

"Well, you're workin' it. For a lander, at least."

"Thanks," Jinto said modestly, followed by a slightly uncomfortable silence.

"Are the Abh really as pretty as they say?" Dorin asked. "I've only ever seen them in holograms."

"Don't know," Jinto said. "I've never seen one up close, either."

"But you went to an Abh school."

At first perplexed, he finally deciphered his friend's misunderstanding. "Yes, I went to an Abh language and culture school, but there were no Abh students, nor even Abh teachers. The school's goal is to educate citizen candidates, and the teachers are all former citizens who aren't genetically Abh. For example, the founder and the headmistress are both divorced women; they're former territorial citizens of Rue Lef Dreuhynu Vorlak. But even though they're Imperial citizens, they're not related to the Frybar or Count Vorash's family in any way. It's simply a private school under the jurisdiction of the territorial government's education department."

"Oh, I thought it was an Imperial establishment."

"Nope. Why would the Abh ever give money to a lander school?"

"That makes sense." Dorin nodded. "Wait—then why'd you come to Delktou instead of going to an Abh school? Knowing Delktou's language won't help you at all."

"The Abh don't have primary schools. So, if you're not a super genius and you don't speak Abh, there's no point trying to go to an Abh high school."

"How do the Abh learn to read and write then?" Durin asked.

"The same way they learn how to speak—from their parents."

The Abh definitely wouldn't allow landers to educate their children in their most formative years. Because their society was intrinsically hierarchical, the Abh emphasized family traditions (Jhedirl). In order to retain those traditions, it was important for parents to conduct primary education.

Thus, the Abh devoted themselves to educating their young children. Nobles who held Ribeun hired representatives (Toserl), and even Lef took time off from their duties to model successors in their own image.

Automated teaching computers (Onwarele) worked with Abh children to fill in any gaps in teachings, and they instituted training camp outings to teach the children valuable social skills.

"Mine was an unusual education," Jinto explained. "Since my father is Count Hyde—I mean, Dreu Haider—I needed to learn the Abh language and culture, but he couldn't teach it to me. He doesn't even understand it himself. That's why they sent me to the most accessible school for Rue Lef candidates."

"And it took seven years?" Dorin laughed. "I always thought you were smart, but maybe you're not the sharpest pencil in the box after all."

"I couldn't even speak Delktou's language for half of the first year I was here!"

"Well, we are a barbaric people on a squalid, rustic Aith," Dorin said facetiously.

"You'd actually believe that, if you ever saw Martine. The very best buildings on Delktou are no match for a Martinese complex," Jinto boasted.

"Even this tower?" Dorin countered, slightly malevolently.

Point, Dorin, Jinto conceded mentally. Due to anti-Abh resistance on Martine, there would be no construction of an orbital tower like those surrounding most planets of the Frybar. The Martinese still had to rely on dangerous and costly Frash to board spaceships. Consequently, there were fewer Martinese volunteers for space travel.

"This tower is absurdly huge," Jinto finally said.

"Yes, everything's bigger in Delktou," Dorin said proudly. "Hey, that lady's checking you out again."

Exasperated, Jinto mussed his brown locks. "It's my hair." Running the gamut from aqua to near-purple, Abh hair was invariably blue.

"Maybe you should dye it. It couldn't be that hard."

"You know, I thought about that. Decided against it."

"Why?"

"For one thing, I don't want to forget who I am. If I dyed my hair, I might start to think I'm a real Abh, in spite of my lander genes."

"You have another reason?"

"Just stubborn, I guess. I may be Rue Sif, but I don't want them to think I'm happy about it."

"Makes sense," Dorin consented. Leaning on the table, he suddenly sported a look of uncharacteristic seriousness. "Hey, if you change your mind and want to escape nobility, I'll help you. This might be your last chance to back out, you know."

"I can resign at any time," Jinto replied.

"But they'll totally cut off your allowance! I could get you a job."

"How? You're just a student."

"I know a manager who understands working students. Actually, he's my uncle. But, you're smart—you could probably get a scholarship or something."

"Thanks, but it's okay," Jinto said. "I want to see the Abh world. Find out what kind of people invaded us."

"Yeah, *that* makes sense," Dorin said, his tone implying the opposite.

"Besides," Jinto continued, "it's not like I'm leaving a lot of friends behind here. You're the only one who came to see me off."

"Well . . ." Dorin had nothing else to say.

"If I ever live as a territorial citizen, I'll come here to Delktou, but I'd definitely need to wait until things calm down. As Jinto Linn, I had friends, but after everyone found out I'd been omitting a couple of titles from my name, no one would give me the time of day. So, thanks for understanding."

Humbly, Dorin smiled and said, "It's a good test to see who your real friends are."

"Yeah, no kidding," Jinto agreed. "If I ever need a favor here, I know who to ask."

"Just leave it to me," Dorin quipped. "After school, I'm going to start a business. I'm sure I can make room for a file clerk when you get back."

"Thanks."

Dorin glanced at the room's huge, ceiling-mounted clock. "Which ship are you boarding? Don't you need go?"

"I'm on a Frybar Wikreurl."

"No way!" A pause. "You know I have no idea what that means, right?"

Jinto laughed. "It's a warship. New students get to travel with the Frybar's war fleet. I was nervous about it at first, but, if I'm going to be a Lodair, I may as well see what it's like."

"And this 'Wikreurl' is coming to this spaceport?" Dorin asked.

"Not sure. Somebody is coming to get me at eighteen hundred hours. That's why I wore these clothes; I'll stick out, so they can find me easily."

"So, an Abh soldier is coming here?"

Jinto shrugged. "I don't know if he'll be Abh or not, but a Labule officer is coming to get me soon."

"I better get out of here, then."

"You're not going to wait until they take me away?"

"And let them see me cry like a baby?" Dorin joked, standing up. "Not a chance."

Rising, Jinto teased back, "Tears from the most notorious villain on Delktou."

"Oh, stop it. You're embarrassing me." Dorin offered his hand, and Jinto grasped it. "What's your formal name, again?"

"Linn Syun-Rock Jarluk Dreu Haider Jinto. I think."

"You're not even sure about your own name?"

"It seems like somebody else's."

"Well, Linn something-something Jinto, remember my name—Ku Dorin. Compared to yours, it shouldn't be that hard."

"How could I forget you? Don't worry about the titles—I'll always just be Linn Jinto, okay?"

"Whatever you say, Linn Syun-Rock Jarluk Dreu Haider Jinto," Dorin recited, proud of his astute memory.

Jinto smiled and let go of Dorin's hand.

"Do your best, man," Dorin advised.

"You, too. Start that business. I may need a job someday."

"Aye-aye, sir," Dorin barked before saluting smartly and leaving. As he exited the lounge and disappeared into an ascent-tube, Dorin never looked back.

Taking his seat again, Jinto noticed the middle-aged woman had found something else to stare at.

Following her line of sight, Jinto saw a slender figure enter the room. Clad in a black Sorf and crimson belt (Wev), the figure walked toward Jinto, the mere sight sending a chill down his spine.

The long arm of the Rue Labule had come for him.

2 **Pilot Trainee (Bene Lodair)**

According to Imperial law (Rue Razem), the Imperial family (Fasanzoerl), nobles, and Lef all fell into the broader category of "Abh." Thus, Jinto (the legitimate progeny of a count) was undeniably Abh by at least one definition.

However, "Abh" had also come to be associated with a particular breed of genetically engineered people. In this respect, Jinto was clearly not Abh. Though they originated from Earth humans, the Abh were inarguably an entirely different species.

Never satisfied, the Abh continued to tinker with the genes of their children to prevent hereditary ailments and guarantee racial unity. They meticulously specified more than twenty-seven thousand nucleotide pairs in each child's DNA before the kid ever saw the light of day.

This scrupulous rigidity carried over into their arts as well. For example, Abh poetry was all fixed-form. The Abh claimed structural limitations made their art more refined. Although there was less room for originality, all Abh art was noticeably spectacular.

Likewise, the strict structural limitations of offspring creation produced few colossal disappointments. Abh children were manufactured to their parents' aesthetic tastes, which were similar to many land worlds' (Nahen) general conception of beauty. Mostly.

Thus, Abh people were conspicuously beautiful, and the officer who came to retrieve Jinto was no exception.

She wore a simple military Alpha that kept her long, blue hair in check. Thin but distinct eyebrows formed perfect arches across her pale forehead. An elegant nose rested above plump but firm lips. And those eyes! Her irises were lapis lazuli blue.

She sported a crimson Wev—the sign of a Lodair.

Jinto struggled to determine her age.

It was incredibly difficult to guess an Abh's age from outward appearance alone. During Zaroth, the stage of development from birth until the age of fifteen, the Abh matured like regular people. After that, from the beginning of their Feroth stage, their appearance matured only ten more years. The entire process took approximately twenty-five years. The Abh never showed any physical indications of aging beyond twenty-five.

Though eternally young, the Abh were not immortal. The imperfect nerve cells from which they manufactured their children eventually led to incurable confusion. When their brains quit working, even the Abh could not escape death.

Eternally proud, the Abh arranged for their respiratory systems to stop before their intellect ceased functioning. However, this only occurred after at least two hundred years.

When all was said and done, an Abh who looked to be in his mid-twenties could be anywhere from forty to two hundred and forty years old.

But there was no mistaking the age of this Lodair. She was either in the very end of her Zaroth period, or the very beginning of her Feroth period. She was probably about the same age as Jinto.

Upon closer inspection, Jinto was convinced of the Lodair's age, but gender was harder to guess. Instinct told him the officer was a *she*, but he couldn't be sure.

Often, Abh men looked like young, beautiful women. And with Abh youth, it was almost impossible to tell.

Parting the sea of people with her (*his?*) tangible sense of importance, the Abh trainee approached Jinto, walking briskly, gracefully.

Pretentiously, Jinto directed his attention to the rank insignia on the breast of the officer's black uniform (Serlin). It was an inverted isosceles triangle, but with curved sides. In the center of the triangle there was a roaring, silver Gaftonosh, which was simultaneously the coat of arms of the Imperial family (Ajh) and the national badge (called the Nigla) of the Frybar. All the signs indicated this was a Lodair Gariar — a flight officer. There were no other decorations on the insignia.

So, she's a Bene Lodair? A pilot trainee?

Like Jinto, she wasn't yet official. After graduating, this Abh would still need to complete a six-month apprenticeship on a Wikreurl or base (Lonid).

A typical teenager, Jinto couldn't help noticing the bosom beneath the insignia. It was just large enough for him to confirm that this Lodair was, in fact, a female.

As she walked toward him, Jinto contemplated meeting her in the middle. Nerves got the best of him, and his feet stayed rooted in his spot.

Violating traditional boundaries of personal space, the pilot trainee came very close to Jinto before she stopped. "Linn Syun-Rock Jarluk Dreu Haider Jinto Lonyu?"

Impressed by the fluidity with which she called his formal name, Jinto just nodded.

She brandished her right hand. Instinctively, Jinto took a step back.

The pilot trainee just raised the hand to her tiara in a traditional Abh greeting.

"I've come from the *Gosroth* to get you. You will come with me." Her voice was feminine in pitch, but her tense inflection was more akin to a man's.

Having delivered her message, she promptly turned on her heels and began to walk away, seemingly indifferent to whether Jinto followed.

What kind of welcome is that? Jinto thought, annoyed.

Then again, he hadn't expected much. Although the dictionary definition of the word "lander" (Aibs) didn't have any discriminatory connotations, his textbooks seemed to imply that landers were susceptible to Abh ridicule. At any rate, he was used to being treated differently.

It didn't seem right to Jinto, and he didn't want to be the kind of person who just accepted baseless scorn.

Maybe this pilot trainee thinks she has better things to do than go pick up the son of a lander-born noble, Jinto reasoned. *Nobody on the patrol ship wanted to do it, so they dumped it on the lowest apprentice. That's why she's so grouchy.*

Jinto knew from personal experience on Delktou that the beginning of a relationship was crucial. And now he felt uneasy, not even knowing this girl's name.

"Um . . . Hey, you!" Jinto called after the pilot trainee.

"What?" She turned around.

"You know my name, but I don't know yours. I'm not sure how it works with the Abh, but it's freaking me out."

The girl's eyes went from big to huge.

Uh-oh. Was that extremely rude? Jinto fretted. He studied Abh culture in school, but maybe they left out some important points of etiquette.

"You can call me Lafiel!" she replied, bursting into a huge grin. She puffed out her chest, as if she'd just won a

fight. The motion caused her hair and the function crystal
(Kos Kisegal) on the ends of her connections chains (Kiseg)
to sway.

Whoa. What was that all about? Jinto was suspicious. *I
just asked her name.*

"But, in exchange for that," she continued, "I want to
call you just Jinto. Okay?"

The sincerity of Lafiel's expression was like boiling
water melting snow—Jinto couldn't stay upset. Her
beautiful eyes actually looked scared that he might deny
her request.

"O-of course," Jinto nodded vehemently. "I prefer
that, anyway."

"Well then, Jinto," said Lafiel, "Let's go."

"Okay." This time he obediently followed her.

"It's my turn to ask you a question, Jinto."

"Shoot."

"Why did you step away when I saluted you?"

"Old habit," Jinto lied. "That's . . . uh . . . how we greet
each other on my home world."

"Peculiar." Lafiel bought it. "It looked like you thought
I was going to hit you. The greetings on your home world
are very strange."

"Anything unfamiliar can seem strange," Jinto
reasoned.

"Yes. I was raised Abh, so I know little about other
cultures."

"Makes sense."

"But you're Abh too, Jinto. You'd better get used to the
Kasarl Gereulak way of doing things."

Jinto secretly groaned. From time to time, the Abh
called themselves Kasarl Gereulak—Kin of the Stars—very
proudly. Why the Abh chose to associate themselves with
giant lumps of burning gas, Jinto couldn't say.

But he could say, "Easier said than done. There are many years of upbringing to unlearn. It'll be hard now."

Jinto sighed, inviting sympathy. His first encounter with the Abh had gone better than he could have expected; he was on a first-name basis with a beautiful girl who was about the same age he was. He'd have to be dead to not be stoked about *that*.

They reached tube number twenty-six.

Using her Kreuno, Lafiel opened the door, revealing a hundred people's worth of seats occupied by about ten.

"What was the ship's name again?" Jinto wanted to keep the friendly conversation alive.

"Gosroth."

"That's right. What Byr does the *Gosroth* belong to?"

"It belongs to the Byr Kureyal."

Ah, the training fleet. "Does that mean there are a lot of pilot trainees like you on board?"

"Are you serious?" she asked incredulously.

Jinto blinked. "You know, it was all I could do just to learn the language. Anything you can tell me about military relationships would be most helpful."

"Oh, I see." Lafiel's face darkened briefly. "I will forgive you."

Man. Is that the Abh idea of an apology?

The Feretocork stopped, having taken them up two floors. As they exited, Jinto noticed there were no civilian passengers on this floor, only uniformed workers.

"There are Klejaga that belong to the training fleet," Lafiel explained as she stepped off the platform. "But training ships are for Kenyu. There are no other Bene Lodair aboard like me. The training fleet also has one more responsibility—to break in new ships. The *Gosroth* was only put into service two months ago. Right now, the Sarerl and crew are practicing maneuvers."

The captain and crew are practicing? That seemed like something to be worried about. "Really?"

"There's nothing to worry about," Lafiel said flatly. "That's a figure of speech. They're all skilled Souk, so the ship's not going to fall apart when you come aboard."

"I wasn't worried," Jinto fibbed.

The wall next to the Dobroria narrowed, making a graceful donut-shaped corridor. Circling around the tube, there was a corridor that led out, where two non-Abh crew members (Sash) stood guard. Many crew members who were non-commissioned officers came from land worlds.

The men saluted. One of them spoke. "Bene, I must inspect your Kreuno, but only because it's a rule."

Lafiel held out her left hand with the Kreuno on it.

The crewmember used a rectangular instrument to read the display on the wristband. "Thank you, Bene. Okay, Lonyu, you're up."

"Of course." Jinto extended his left hand.

The crewmember clearly wondered why a lander like Jinto was a noble, but all the same, he checked Jinto's identity quietly. "All clear, Lonyu. Please pass through."

"Thank you," Lafiel said, prodding Jinto through the passage.

Once they were inside the corridor, it began to move along a track. Glancing at the words "Bore Rue Labule" (which meant Imperial Star Force-controlled area) scrawled on the wall, Jinto shivered. On Delktou, the military was something they only read about in history books. Now, he was both literally and metaphorically entering this mysterious organization.

At the end of the automatic track, there was a door. The door opened by itself as Jinto and Lafiel neared. A black spaceship waited just beyond the door.

"Is that the *Gosroth?*" Jinto asked.

"You're not serious, are you?" Lafiel looked at him sharply.

"I'm ignorant, remember?" Jinto meekly excused his error.

"Yes, but I thought there was a limit to ignorance."

"Now that you mention it, the Rebisath I flew on a long time ago was a little bigger."

"I don't know what class that was, but that ship was certainly much, much bigger than this. This is the *Gosroth's* embarkation shuttle. We call it a Kalique. It transports Bosnal when the ship can't enter port directly. It's also used to make contact with other ships. Although it can hold fifty passengers, today there's just one."

"What an honor." *Does that mean she's going to fly this thing?* Jinto panicked; he had a preconceived notion of spaceship pilots (Sedraleia) that didn't include girls his own age. Jinto didn't want to risk wounding his budding relationship with the girl, nor did he want to provoke her.

"Where are you going to sit?" she asked.

"It looks like there's only one seat . . ."

"The copilot's seat is open, if you want. Or would you prefer the rear residence area?"

"Is there a beautiful flight attendant?" Jinto asked, tweaking an eyebrow.

"No," Lafiel said very seriously, "but there's a beautiful Sedraleia. Now make up your mind."

"Of course I'll sit in the copilot's seat." Jinto swallowed his fear and put his life in her hands.

3 Daughter of Love (Fryum Neg)

"What's Frokaj like, anyway?" Jinto asked as he checked (and double-checked) his safety restraints.

"It's hard to explain, no matter how I phrase it." Lafiel extended the Kiseg on her Alpha and connected them to the back of her seat.

Frokaj, a legitimate sixth sense, was unique to the Abh, originating from a spatial-sense organ (Frosh) only present in Abh frontal lobes. The tiara, in addition to being an indicator of rank, was an indispensable tool to the Abh. It allowed particles to carry messages directly from a ship's sensors into Abh brains.

And when not connected to a ship, the Alpha functioned as an environmental radar, scanning the space surrounding its wearer.

Jinto realized that when they'd first met, he'd misconstrued Lafiel's actions. When she walked away from him, he thought she didn't care whether or not he followed. In truth, she sensed him perfectly with her Frokaj!

"Is it true you know everything going on in the ship?" Jinto probed.

"Yes," Lafiel stated. "You can't possibly find it that interesting."

Jinto shrugged. "Until now, I've never met anybody with Frokaj."

"Interesting," Lafiel said. "I can't imagine life without Frokaj. I still can't explain it, though. How do you describe hearing to the deaf?"

"Right. So, are you calculating the orbit now?"

"Calculate orbit?" Lafiel asked, then bit her lower lip. "No, I don't do that."

"Oh. So you just get the numerical values, then." Apparently, he overestimated the Abh's field of navigation (Rilbido).

"I don't process any numerical values."

"Then how do you work out the orbit?"

"I just do it. When you throw something, aim is instinctual, right? It's the same as that. The calculations are subconscious."

Jinto frowned. "Is your aim ever . . . off?"

"Only children miss. Don't worry."

He *had* to worry. "Oh. I see."

Jinto looked around the cockpit (Shirsh Sediar) for something to distract himself.

Odd. I thought there would be a lot more to it than this.

The cockpit was hemispherical. There were display screens in front of his chair, but he couldn't discern any instruments or steering equipment. There was just a smooth, white wall.

As far as Jinto could tell, the only navigational equipment was attached to the seats in the form of a few control buttons (called Borsh) on the right armrest of the chair. It didn't make sense to Jinto that the complex and delicate operation of piloting a spaceship was possible with this sparse setup.

Wait. Is that a Gooheik?

Although he'd learned of the glove controls in his Abh classes, Jinto had never seen one, nor thought them was very practical—how could a person fly a ship using only voice commands and finger movements? Yet there it was, resting on the left side of the chair: an elbow-length glove with a metallic index finger.

"Don't you think that's a dangerous way to steer a ship?" Jinto asked, as Lafiel slid her hand into the Gooheik.

"Why would I think that?"

"I mean," Jinto said, "don't you ever forget you're wearing that thing and, I don't know, scratch your head or something?"

"When connected to the ship, I forget that my left hand even exists," Lafiel replied.

"That's crazy. The interstellar spaceships landers fly are definitely more . . ." He wanted to say practical, but decided to be more tactful. "Well, the navigation equipment is derived from different ideas, that's all."

"This," Lafiel indicated her left arm, "is far superior."

"But the movements are all so minute. Don't you ever mess up?"

"Do you mess up walking?"

Jinto said nothing.

"That's what it's like when I fly a ship. I just think about what I want the ship to do, and my fingers move themselves."

"Wow. You must have had some pretty intense training."

She blinked. "I've had this ability since I was a child. It's not something you train for."

"Oh," Jinto peeped, feeling understandably inferior.

"Is it okay if we leave now?" Lafiel asked.

"Anytime."

And just like that, the screen lit up. Baronh poured across it at high speeds.

"Can you read all that? I mean, that fast?" Jinto tried to read it, but it was whizzing past so quickly that he couldn't make out a single word of it. It just gave him a headache.

"I don't read it," Lafiel admitted.

"Then why have it at all?"

"The Dateyukil inspects the vessel. Any irregularities pop up on the screen in large red text, long enough to read. It's also for ambiance. Doesn't it look nice?"

At last, the rapid-fire string of words stopped. The screen cleared before blinking a large "Gosnoh," which was the Abh word for "everything's A-OK."

"It's done." She nodded to herself.

"It's so easy."

"Yeah. The computer crystal does all that work for me."

"But machines make mistakes." Try as he might, Jinto could not convince himself this was safe.

"People make mistakes, too."

"Thanks. I feel much better now."

"You're such a worry-wort. We're not going very far at all."

"How far is it?"

Lafiel sighed. "That's the wrong question. They're moving, too. If you meant what is the difference in amplitude, then the answer is about five Sedarjh."

Sedarjh were derived from ancient Earth measurements, and one Sedarjh was equal to exactly one thousand kilometers. So, they would be crossing at least five thousand kilometers of nothingness during their trip from the spaceport (Bidaut) to the *Gosroth*.

That distance probably seemed like nothing to the Karsal Gereulak, but Jinto found it unsettling.

Lafiel, however, didn't even notice. The Bene moved her left hand deftly and the Gosnoh message on the screen disappeared. In its place appeared the body of a spaceport worker.

"Belysega," Lafiel greeted him, addressing the Space Traffic Controller.

"Planet Delktou's Spaceport Control number one!" the man barked.

"*Gosroth's* embarkation Kalique. Command Number 0100937684. Please decompress military dock number two."

"Roger, wilco. Decompressing . . . now!"

Jinto wished he could see what was happening outside the Shirsh Sediar; although he'd been on a ship before, he hardly remembered it.

"Can you tell what's happening outside?" Jinto asked, hoping Lafiel might be able to display their surroundings on the screen.

"Of course. Do you want to see it?"

"Yeah! I don't have Frokaj, you know."

"Oh, right," Lafiel sounded almost sympathetic for a moment. "Okay. Here goes."

Except for the screen and the ship's banner (Guraw Mongarl), the walls disappeared. They were still there, of course, but the ship processed its surroundings and displayed the outside as a hologram.

From a visual standpoint, atmospheric decompression disappointed Jinto. Nothing seemed to be happening. After a minute, the controller informed them that decompression was finished.

"Please open the Soyuth to military dock number two," Lafiel requested.

"Roger, *Gosroth* embarkation Kalique."

Upon these words, a huge door opened in front of them, revealing an endless sea of stars.

"Completely open, confirmed. Request permission to leave port."

"Permission granted, *Gosroth* embarkation Kalique. Do you want electromagnetic catapult?"

"Not necessary. We'll use low-temperature jet propulsion." She turned to Jinto. "The electromagnetic catapult would really send you for a loop."

Jinto was sure it would.

"We wish you a safe journey, *Gosroth* embarkation Kalique. Planet Delktou Spaceport Control number one, out."

"Thank you. *Gosroth* embarkation Kalique, out."

Immediately after the controller's image disappeared from the screen, Lafiel's fingers began to dance through the air. With a small amount of vibration, the ship began to rise off the floor.

Concerned that they might hit the ceiling of the dock, Jinto tried to look up. It didn't seem to concern Lafiel, whose eyes were closed. Jinto knew she was concentrating her Frokaj, but he wished she'd do it with her eyes open.

Ultimately, his anxiety was needless.

The ship began to ascend. With miraculous timing, it entered the vacuum of space just before it would have crashed into the ceiling.

Jinto felt his body try to escape from his chair. Apparently, they were out of the range of the artificial gravity (Wameroth) applied to the orbital tower.

Good thing for this Apyuf, he thought. *Without a seat belt, I might have floated away.*

"You're amazing," Jinto praised her sincerely.

Lafiel pouted. "A child could fly this ship."

"Well," he said, feeling insulted, "I don't know how old you are. It's rude to ask a lady."

"Are you implying I look like a child?" she shot back with a sharp glance.

"Don't be ridiculous," Jinto sighed. *Ruining this girl's mood seems like it might be the easiest thing to do in the universe.* "It's just . . . um . . . hard to tell how old you people are."

She cheered up. "I just turned sixteen this year. I'm pretty young."

A year younger than I am?

"Why is it rude?" she asked suddenly.

"What?"

"To ask a lady her age. I don't understand why that's rude."

Jinto paused; although he'd always heard this to be true, no one had ever bothered to tell him why. "Probably because women hope to look younger than they are. At least the women on Delktou and Martine."

"Peculiar. I wonder why."

"I'm certainly no expert. If you want the right answer, try asking a lander woman." Jinto shifted in his seat, then tried to change the subject. "Are all pilot trainees as young as you?"

"The Kenru exams aren't that difficult—if you haven't passed them by the time you're eighteen, you shouldn't try." Lafiel beamed childishly. "However, very few are accepted for enrollment at age thirteen. Not to brag."

"Well," Jinto was taken with her competitiveness, "not to brag myself, but I've entered the Kenru Sazoir at seventeen, despite having to learn two foreign languages first."

"That's incredible," she said with true admiration.

BEEP! BEEP! BEEP!

"What was that?" The beeps echoed in Jinto's ear like an alarm clock.

"We're clear to accelerate now." Lafiel casually gestured with the Gooheik.

"Oh. Great! How long until we arrive?"

"This ship doesn't have a Wameria, so it depends how much G-force you can handle."

Knowing Abh standard gravity was only about half that of Planet Delktou's, Jinto replied coolly, "I'm a lander. If you can take it, I'm sure I can, too."

"Okay. Then it's only going to take seven minutes. So, here we go." As soon as Lafiel said that, Jinto was smashed against his seat.

He felt like someone really fat was standing on his stomach, crushing his insides.

"What's happening?" he managed to eke out.

"It's Kaimukoth," Lafiel said, unfazed. "Didn't they teach you about acceleration?"

"Yes. Yes! But so much . . ." He could hardly get the words out. The force was crushing his blood vessels, chafing his limbs, and pressing on his bladder. Jinto estimated he could tolerate the sensation for one minute at most. Seven would be preposterous, possibly lethal. "Y-you're fine?"

"Of course. Our ancestors didn't have Wameria, so they configured our bodies to accommodate both high gravitational force and weightlessness. My frame and circulatory system have . . ."

"Please, Lafiel, slow it down."

"Okay, but it will take longer."

"Whatever. Please . . ."

"I suppose it can't be helped." The ship's velocity decreased. "Hm. I had to adjust the course. We need to go slightly faster. Can you take it?"

"I don't know. Can you do it without killing me?"

"Let's find out." Lafiel resumed conducting an invisible orchestra with her left hand, and the ship began to accelerate again. Jinto felt heavier than normal, but not nauseated or uncomfortable. *I could probably even walk around.*

"That better?" she asked.

"Much, thanks. How much acceleration is this?"

"Four units of standard gravity. That amount of Daemon is the normal acceleration for flights with landers on board. For a longer journey, we cut it to two Daemon, because that's comparable to Nahen gravity in most cases."

"I wish you had warned me it would be so intense. That's a lot for a lander to deal with," Jinto said enviously.

"I thought you could take it," Lafiel said, no trace of mocking in her voice.

"I guess I'm flattered by your overestimation."

"Well, you're not a lander. You're Abh."

"I sure don't feel like it. I mean, genetically, I'm one hundred-percent lander." The legal definition of Abh couldn't change heredity. If the definition of "birds" was legally changed to include swine, pigs still couldn't fly.

"In spite of your genes," Lafiel replied, "you'd better start *thinking* Abh. Rue Sif don't lose their composure from high acceleration."

"I'll keep that in mind," Jinto acquiesced meekly.

The whole acceleration episode made it clear to Jinto that he was not cut out to be an Imperial noble. *Maybe I should ask her to turn this thing around, and go see if Dorin has a job for me yet.*

But Jinto knew that he couldn't go back.

After a while, the ship decelerated, and then there were a few sensational seconds of complete weightlessness. Planet Delktou floated overhead, now just a ball of blue and white, making Jinto feel like he was falling into infinity.

"Say," Jinto asked, "what's your social position?"

"Why do you ask?" Lafiel snapped back.

"I don't know." Jinto was flustered; he hoped she didn't misconstrue his innocent curiosity as an attempt to show off his own noble status. "I was just wondering why you joined the Labule, even though you're so young. I thought maybe you wanted to get your Star Force duties out of the way early, like me. Was I wrong to ask?"

"No, but I don't really want to tell you. As long as I'm in uniform, there's nothing to indicate my pedigree, at least until I become a Sedraleia."

An Imperially appointed pilot? Impressive. "So, social status has no relationship to the Labule?"

"Correct." She nodded. "In the military, this is the only rank we honor." Lafiel pointed to the insignia on her sleeve.

"Got it. Back to the other question — why did you enlist? Is it duty, or a personal decision?"

"It is my duty," Lafiel acknowledged.

"Aha!" Military duty wasn't imposed on Imperial citizens. For them, being able to enroll in the Kenru was an option, not a responsibility. Jinto was fairly certain Lafiel was a nobleman's daughter. "Thought so."

"What?"

"Nothing." Jinto clammed up. His first impression of Lafiel made Jinto suspect that she came from the upper echelon. He tried to decide if it would be worse to voice his suspicions or to keep quiet.

"It's not just duty," Lafiel admitted.

"Then why?"

"I wanted to grow up quickly."

"Right." An officer is considered an adult, regardless of age. "What's the rush? Being a kid was great."

Lafiel thought about this for a minute, then abruptly asked, "Do you have a birth secret?"

" 'Birth secret'?" Jinto had no idea what that meant. "No, I don't. My mother died when I was very small." He hoped this adequately explained his lack of a birth secret, whatever it was.

"Your mother? I thought you were your father's child. Aren't you Lonyu Dreu Haider's son?"

"Yes, he's my father. Oh . . . right." Jinto recalled hearing that Abh, unlike landers, didn't marry. There were couples — people who loved each other and lived together — in Abh society. And sometimes, these relationships lasted long enough to resemble marriages, but a " 'til death do you part" arrangement was extremely rare.

The Abh were more likely to burn with passion, hot and quick enough to drive themselves crazy. Like incinerators, the fires of Abh love left little behind.

Because they tended not to remain coupled for long, the Abh had no real concept of what it meant to have a pair of parents. This necessitated special Abh words like "Fryum Loran" and "Fruk Saran." Respectively, these terms literally translate to "female whose parent is male," and "male whose parent is female."

"You've heard of marriage, right?" Jinto asked.

"That's right. You're a lander. I keep forgetting."

"Ha. Yes, I was born from a marriage. So, I'm both my father's and my mother's son."

"Strange." Lafiel habitually tilted her head when she pondered something foreign. "What's it like to have two parents? Were you sad when you mother died?"

Though the questions were simple and direct, Jinto was surprised; he immediately thought of Lena Clint, not his birth mother, whom he had only ever seen in holograms. "Yes. I was sad."

"Forgive me," Lafiel said, turning away. "That was a stupid question."

"No, it's fine. I really don't remember her very well, because she died when I was very young."

"That's terrible," Lafiel said, seemingly envious that he ever had two parents, "but it isn't a birth secret."

"Why not?"

"Both of your Larliin were in your family, so there was no secret about your birth, was there?"

"There could be." Jinto wondered about it. "I'm not sure about other land worlds, but on Martine and Delktou, sometimes people become parents without wanting to. Other times, people can't be parents even if they try and try. It seems like there's a lot of room for birth secrets with those situations."

"What do you mean?" Lafiel was confused.

"Look into it sometime. It's really hard to find out how and why you came to be." Seeing she was still stupefied, he said, "Never mind. What's your birth secret, and does it have anything to do with why you've joined the military?"

"My birth secret. Right." She looked around as if to confirm their seclusion. "I don't know whether or not I was a Fryum Neg."

"Fryum Neg?" Jinto asked. *Is that some kind of religious concept? No, no. The Abh are atheists.* "I don't know what that is. My education seems to have a few holes in it," Jinto excused himself.

It was true, though. Although it was an Abh language and culture school, the lessons primarily focused on the langauge. Any curriculum pertaining to culture concerned proper manners and etiquette for Rue Lef. While the teachers' explanations of the Abh government and law would have stood up in legal documents, their elucidations of Abh daily life had been ambiguous and conspicuously implausible.

The Abh were partly to blame for Jinto's poor education; though they weren't secretive about their culture, they were decidedly unenthusiastic about explaining it. Because the teachers were just temporary employees of the Abh, they had no more inside perspective than the students. The few books available on the subject were all written by former Lef. Authors who never once left Delktou wrote page after page of nonsense and irresponsible conjecture.

Jinto wracked his brain for an educated guess at the meaning of "Fryum Neg."

"Does that mean you don't know how your parents made you?" Jinto suddenly felt rather uncomfortable. "Uh, I mean, the Abh are famous for not marrying, but, well, how do they make children?" Perhaps he was treading on thin ice with this topic.

Lafiel was amused, not offended. "You don't know where Abh babies come from?"

"Well, not exactly." Jinto blushed. *Damn. The last thing I need is a younger girl to explain the birds and bees to me.* "I know you don't conceive inside your bodies."

"Sometimes we do."

"Really? But what about the uh . . . the genetic . . . uh inspection? You know, the Janarlmukos?"

"Doesn't happen until after the fertilization of the egg. We usually transfer them to Janyu, but sometimes a woman wants the unique, personal experience of carrying the embryo in her own womb."

"Oh." Rumor on Delktou had it that Abh women didn't have wombs. *One fallacy down the drain!*

"There are two types of conception using Janyu."

"Right." Jinto nodded. "I think I'm in over my head, here. From what I've heard, your whole race probably has birth secrets. My books made it sound like you could make children from one person's DNA, or from the genes of two people of the same sex, or from two relatives. I just wonder what stories I'll hear—"

"Yes, we practice all those methods," Lafiel interrupted.

Jinto's jaw dropped.

"It's a parent's choice whose genes he wants to use to create his child. If he deems his own sufficient, then he doesn't need to use anyone else's. But there's always room for improvement, so parents usually decide to mix in the genes of others."

"Weird." Jinto was confused. "But there's such an emphasis on an hereditary pecking order. I mean, your blood relatives aren't necessarily of the same pedigree!"

"The inheritance of Jhedirl, not genes, is important."

"But . . ." The more he thought about it, the more it made sense that the Abh, who genetically engineered their children, ignored bloodlines. It was all about tradition.

"The most common way of making a child is to combine your genes with those of someone you love."

"Now that sounds familiar." He relaxed.

"Of course, the person may be of the same sex, a relative, or, in some cases, multiple people. For some reason, this usually makes landers uncomfortable." Lafiel looked at Jinto questioningly.

"It does," Jinto affirmed. "So weird."

"It's not that strange; genetic engineering is not unique to the Abh."

"On the world I'm from, we're not exactly enamored of gene tampering."

"I can see that," Lafiel snarled. "Sorry to snap, but this isn't exactly something you talk about with a person you just met."

Making a conscious effort to remain composed, Jinto apologized. A moment passed while he entertained the possibility that the Abh weren't so different after all.

"Saying 'I want your genes' is the most serious confession of love."

Lafiel said the words like a little girl reading a fairy tale, Jinto noticed.

Maybe that's the Abh equivalent of a marriage proposal.

"When that statement leads to the conception of a child, that child is —"

"A Fryum Neg." Jinto figured it out.

"Exactly. Although, technically, a boy would be called a Fruk Neg."

So that's what an Abh birth secret is like.

"Well, maybe you could ask your parent." Jinto gulped. "Unless . . . He's not . . ."

She faced him. "My father is alive and well. He'll be chasing women for another two hundred years, at the rate he's going."

Jinto hadn't expected such a candid response. "Then why don't you try asking him?"

"Do you think I haven't thought of that?"

Eyes fixed to the floor, Jinto shook his head.

"My father wouldn't tell me." Just talking about it made Lafiel's face darken with anger. "He subscribes to the belief that birth secrets build character."

"Maybe you could do some research."

"When I become an adult, I'll gain access to my genetic records. But until then, I'd need his permission."

"Ah." At last Jinto understood. She wanted to become an adult quickly in order to solve her own genetic mystery.

"It's silly of him to hide it. Unless it's something really terrible that needs to be kept a secret!" She paused to calm down. "I always thought he made up a birth secret just to tease me."

"Why would he do that?"

"When I was younger, I always wanted to say I was a Fryum Neg, so I continually pestered him to reveal his

Larliin. He wouldn't budge, but I wore away at him like a river slowly wears away a boulder. One day, he agreed to bring his Larliin home. You know what happened?"

"He didn't do it?"

"Worse. He brought Horia before me and said 'this beautiful creature is responsible for the best parts of your genes.' "

"What's wrong with that?"

"Horia was our pet cat!" Lafiel was genuinely aggravated.

Unable to control himself, Jinto burst out laughing. "And you believed that?"

She gritted her teeth. "It's scientifically possible."

Irritation, not embarrassment. She's so unusual, he thought.

"Really?" Now that he thought about it, the high corners of her eyes did resemble those of a cat. "You people do that kind of thing?"

"It's not legal. It *is* immoral."

"There's one thing we think in common!"

"You're Abh too, Jinto."

"Yeah, I suppose." Jinto couldn't disagree. "But, if it's not legal, why didn't you figure out it was a lie?"

"I was eight years old and ignorant of the law."

"Right." He tried to stifle his chortling.

She sighed. "I mean, Horia was a good cat, but who wants cat genes? I cried all night."

"I understand where you're coming from. Maybe."

"The worst thing for me was thinking my dad was the kind of pervert who'd procreate with a cat!" While she spoke, Lafiel gesticulated wildly with her right hand, which made Jinto incredibly nervous.

But her left hand, still in the Gooheik, was steady as a rock, as if paralyzed.

"For a long time, I thought I might grow claws or have glow-in-the dark eyes! Maybe I'd have to start walking on all fours and eating mice."

"Well, at least your doubts are cleared up now."

"Yeah." Lafiel nodded. "But I'll never forget those days of anxiety. I hope to become an officer quickly and distance myself from my father."

"Do you hate your father?" Jinto asked with trepidation, unsure whether Abh etiquette permitted new acquaintances to ask such a personal question.

"I don't hate him." Lafiel scrunched her beautiful face. "I don't want to acknowledge it, but I love him. I think of him with pride. I do hate being *around* him, from time to time."

Jinto thought of his own father. He'd barely even seen Count Hyde's face in the last seven years, except in the news. Feelings of betrayal and abandonment always accompanied the memories of his dad.

Jinto wanted to say that he felt love for his father. He certainly didn't hate him. He just didn't know what he felt. It was entirely possible that he had repressed all feelings for his father.

"Every family has its problems," Jinto commented. "What changed your mind about you being half-cat? Did you learn something new?"

"Yes." Lafiel brightened. "I did. I found out it's a person I know well. A woman I admire. I actually was a Fryum Neg."

"I'm glad to hear it," Jinto said. He smiled at her.

4 Patrol Ship Gosroth (Resii Gosroth)

Halfway through Jinto's exciting explanation of minchiu and the nuances of its scoring system, Lafiel perked up.

"Jinto," she interrupted. "Look down."

There, seemingly suspended in a sea of twinkling stars, was a ship. Shaped like a flattened hexagon, the ship had numerous cylindrical ports, many of which were open.

"Whoa. Is that the *Gosroth?*" Jinto asked.

"Yes. As you can see, it's slightly bigger than this Kalique," Lafiel said facetiously.

From where they were, Jinto had a hard time grasping the true size of the patrol ship. For all he knew, it could have been as big as a planet or smaller than the Kalique. Jinto agreed with her anyway.

The ship continued to grow as they approached. The Kalique ceased decelerating and weightlessness ensued. From their perspective, the cylindrical ship resembled a runaway turret. Jinto imagined a lonely and forlorn castle, languorously searching the galaxy.

Finally, the Kalique passed the *Gosroth*. Very slowly. As the Kalique crept along the battleship, the visual image gave Jinto the sensation that he was falling from a great height, albeit very gently.

Until that moment, Jinto had seen very few weapons in his life. There were glimpses of Delktou policemen's paralyzer guns (Ribwasia) here and there, but nothing even came close to the magnitude of the military hardware floating before him.

"Wow. It's really amazing." Jinto admired the ship. It blew his mind that something so monstrous could be designed for battle.

"Oh, right. *Now* you're impressed," Lafiel teased.

"It looks different from far away. You wouldn't understand, with your Frokaj and all," he shot back. Noticing a crease in Lafiel's forehead, he laughed. "Please, don't feel sorry for me. Even without Frokaj, I intend to go on living as I have before; strongly, surely, and comfortably cognizant of my lack of Frokaj."

"I see," Lafiel said, looking away. "Well, I'll give you a chance to admire it slowly, then."

"Excellent."

At length, they passed the ship's Imperial medal (Rue Nigla). Similar in design to a rank insignia, the Rue Nigla differed in color; its border and Gaftonosh were gold, and the ground beneath the beast was black. In terms of size, the Rue Nigla was a mountain to the molehill of a rank insignia.

You could play a minchiu match on that thing.

And then, the Kalique passed under the tip of the ship's bow. Lafiel made a minute, circular motion with her wrist, and the vessel slid sideways. Jinto watched the tip of the giant ship swing overhead like the pendulum of some cosmic clock.

"The *Gosroth* is the Frybar's latest model ship," Lafiel explained. "From end to end, it measures twelve point eight two Wethdajh."

"That much, huh?" Jinto would have guessed more, but his concept of Wethdajh was purely theoretical.

"I know. It's small compared to a battle-ready Alek or a commercial Isath. I'm sure the ship you traveled on was bigger than this one. But there's never been a spacecraft with this much battle strength in the history of the Frybar — probably in the history of the universe."

"I'll bet."

Lafiel tilted their vessel to give Jinto a better view of the battleship. "Seen enough?"

"Yeah, thanks."

Lafiel made a movement with her left hand and a male Lodair materialized in front of them, his image suspended among the stars. "Kalique One, Comand Number 0100937684, Duty Number 052201. Requesting reception."

"Roger," the officer replied. "External control ready. What are you looking at out there anyway? Is there something wrong with the ship?" he teased.

"Lonyu Jarluk Dreu wanted to see the difference between a Kalique and a Resii," Lafiel said, glancing at Jinto.

"Weird. Okay, perform Lonjhoth Rirrag."

"Roger." While deftly moving her fingers, Lafiel said to Jinto, "I don't like to use the computer crystal, but it's a military regulation."

Before Jinto could speak, the Lodair butted in. "The Labule isn't dumb enough to give a Bene the opportunity to damage the ship. Concatenation confirmed."

"Confirmed here, too. Please end communication."

"Communication ended." And the officer blipped off the screen. A complicated chart took his place.

"Now, we just wait," Lafiel said, slightly bitter. "It's on autopilot from here on out."

"Oh, thanks."

"Don't thank me; it's my job."

"Speaking of jobs," Jinto began, "what do you do with all your free time? When you aren't piloting the Kalique, I mean."

"It's not like that. A Bene is an apprentice."

"Right . . ."

"That means they can ask me to do anything they'd ask of a Garia Lodair. All the little things add up; I'm very busy."

"I see." Jinto nodded.

"If you become a Bene, you'll be busy, too."

"I'm a Sazoirl."

Lafiel shook her head. "Administrators are busy! Foodstuff and furniture procedures can take all day."

"Oh boy!" Jinto moaned. "I can hardly wait."

Directly in front of them, a hole appeared in the patrol ship. Attitude control caused a slight change in gravity. Jinto's stomach lurched.

Suddenly, the Shirsh Sediar made a quarter turn so the opening was directly below them. The patrol ship's artificial gravity kicked in, and the Kalique began to fall—much faster than Jinto thought was reasonable for a safe landing.

"Oh boy."

At the very last second, the lower attitude-control jets fired, and the shuttle landed gently on the landing deck (Goriaav).

The gate on the ceiling (called a Horl Soyuth) closed, and the lights came on.

The officer from previous communications appeared on the screen and announced the commencement of pressurization.

"Standing by until pressurization is completed," Lafiel responded.

White fog blasted in from all directions, creating a complex swirl that resembled a miniature hurricane.

The fog stopped flowing, settled over the cabin like a haze, then dissipated.

"Pressurization complete. Stand by, please," the Lodair ordered.

"Understood."

"Stand by?" Jinto looked at Lafiel, unsure whether this was normal. "What are we waiting for?"

"Relax. They just need to prepare the Patmsaihoth," Lafiel said as she removed the Gooheik and returned her tiara's Kiseg to their original position.

"Patmsaihoth?" To the best of his recollection, that was some kind of ceremony to welcome important people aboard the ship. "For whom?"

"If you really don't know, you're even dumber than I thought."

"Oh." Jinto knew it was for him, but he hadn't expected them to roll out the red carpet when he enlisted as a mere Sazoirl. "I just thought it was a ceremony for people who are Shewas or above."

"It's for all people with the title of Excellency. Don't forget, you have the Traiga Lonyu now."

"That's right, I do." Jinto smiled. "Is the ceremony really just for me?"

"You're a member of the Voda, Jinto. In the Frybar, noble landers are nothing to sneeze at."

There were, at that time, approximately twenty-five million Abh. Of those, two hundred thousand were Imperial nobles, the majority of whom were Lef. Lef who inhabited planets within their territories were further classified as Voda.

Now, there were about a billion Lef, and almost nine hundred billion territorial citizens (Sos) under the Frybar rule. There were only sixteen thousand Voda—twenty thousand if one generously included their families. Thus, Voda were not terribly common.

Count Hyde's family was definitely a small group.

Jinto swallowed thickly. "Oh man. I've been bad at ceremonies and rituals from day one."

"It's not that big a deal," Lafiel assured him. "The Sarerl will introduce herself, then present the ship's high-ranking Lodair. That's all it is."

"Even so, I'll probably find a way to screw it up . . ."

The left rear door opened. A mechanical contraption (Onhokia) spread a red carpet, and six officers emerged from behind it.

The woman in the front had a tiara with one wing (an Alpha Klabrar) that stretched from her eyebrow to her shoulder-length hair. The wing kept her hair in check, which, Jinto guessed, would keep it out of the way inside a pressurized space helmet (Saput). The commander's cane (Greu) tied to the Kutaroev on the woman's hip suggested she had the rank of captain (Sarerraj).

"Patmsaihoth preparations complete," someone announced. "Lonyu Jarluk Dreu Haider, please join our ship."

"Roger," said Lafiel, nudging Jinto.

"All right." Jinto unhooked his seat belt and stood up. "You coming?"

"Why would I do that?"

"Oh. Right." Jinto despaired. "Will I see you again?"

"The living space is limited—our paths will likely cross," she said simply.

This wasn't exactly the response Jinto hoped to hear, but it would have to do.

"Then, thanks for bringing me this far."

"I enjoyed it."

"Good." He smiled.

Four of the six officers participating in the Patmsaihoth wore the scarlet insignia of Garia. The one farthest to the left was the captain (Sarerl). A military engineer (Skoem) stood directly to her left, and all the way on the end there was a Sazoirl.

Having scrutinized the scene, Jinto wondered what to do. He regretted not asking Lafiel. And he regretted that Delktou's Abh language and culture school left him ill-prepared for a Patmsaihoth.

At the very least, he decided to stand up straight.

A Sash in the distance blew a whistle, and each of the six officers saluted in unison.

Jinto fought the instinct to return the salute; his class on Delktou had instructed him against that. Instead, he awkwardly lined up his heels and bowed his head (keeping his back straight), in accordance with Abh etiquette.

"It's an honor to have you aboard our ship, Lonyu," said the captain. As she spoke, her golden eyes seemed to glow. "I am Bomowas Lexshu, Captain of the Resii Gosroth."

So the Abh also introduce themselves by name? Is this normal? Even for a Hecto-Commander?

Jinto bowed again before launching into his moniker. "I'm Linn Syun-Rock Jarluk Dreu Haider. I'm in your hands, Sarerl, while en route to Arosh." He was pleased that he somehow managed to say his own name without making any mistakes.

"Leave it to me. Allow me to introduce my subordinates."

Although Lexshu bore a moderate resemblance to Lafiel, the rest of the Lodair had unique features, negating Jinto's first impression that Abh appearances lacked individuality. Lexshu commenced naming the new faces.

79

First, she announced a Deca-Commander, Lowas Skem Gumrua. This engineer was responsible for the adjustment and inspection of the ship's machinery, most notably the main engines of the Wikreurl. Her ebony skin stood in stark contrast to her sky-blue eyes.

Next was the ship's clerk, Lowas Sazoir Diesh, who was in charge of monitoring and maintaining the crew's health and wellness. Somehow, his reddish eyes were incredibly calm.

Lowas Reilia was the first mate as well as the senior navigator, Alm Rilbiga. A friendly grin was permanently etched onto his face directly beneath his tidy, blue mustache.

Next, Lexshu introduced the Alm Tlakia — the senior gunnery officer. With eyes like razor blades, the frontline flight officer, Lekle Saryush, eyed Jinto.

Luekule Yunseryua as Alm Drokia acted as the senior communications officer, and she was last in the line. She radiated serenity.

They all appeared to be in their mid-twenties, but since they were Abh, Jinto had absolutely no way to be certain.

"We depart at once," Lexshu said, concluding the introductions. "Will you honor us with your presence on the Gahorl?"

"Gladly," Jinto replied, glancing back to the shuttle behind him. Lafiel had yet to emerge.

"A Sash will retrieve your luggage later," Lexshu assured him, misinterpreting Jinto's look.

"Great. Thanks."

With a gesture, Lexshu beckoned Jinto to follow her. "This way, please."

As if the experience of meeting five high-ranking Lodair weren't already nervewracking enough, they expected Jinto to walk alongside the Sarerl.

On Delktou, Lexshu's beauty would have been without equal. Her golden eyes were disconcerting, but they only augmented her natural charm.

Sure, Jinto had experience interacting with girls—he'd made a point to practice it on Delktou, in his own way. However, older women were still a complete mystery to him—especially gorgeous older women who were commanders of interstellar battleships.

He couldn't get his heart to stop racing.

They walked into the ship's command center. The walls of the room curved slightly as they approached the ceiling. *It must be spherical,* Jinto guessed. At any rate, the center of the room where the captain sat was higher than the outer edges, where the rest of the Lodair worked.

"Lonyu Jarluk Dreu Haider and Sarerl!" the bridge Sash Leitofec announced. Jinto and the captain accepted this as their cue to enter the elevated portion of the room.

There were nine officers present, and they all stood up to salute.

"Show the exterior image, please." Upon Lexshu's command, the wall turned into an infinite field of stars to accommodate for Jinto's lack of Frokaj. The Lodair all connected their tiara's Kiseg.

"Prepare for departure." The Hecto-Commander's voice snapped like a whip.

Seated in his chair above the action, Jinto felt like a mischievous boy who'd stumbled into a forbidden hiding place, perfect for viewing the Lodair at work.

"All engines normal," Lowas Skem Gumrua declared.

"Life support normal," said Lowas Sazoil Diesh.

"Navigational preparations complete." Lekle Saryush put on the Gooheik.

"We're cleared to pass through the Space Traffic Control gate of Count Vorash's nation between the times of

15:27 and 15:27:18," Lekle Yunseryua informed them.

Summing it all up, the second in command, Luse Reilia, said, "Departure preparations complete."

The captain nodded. "Accelerate at six Daemon toward the Sord Vorlak."

"Roger," Lekle Saryush accepted the order. "Heading toward Gate 17-62-55."

"Acknowledged," Lexshu replied quickly.

Thanks to the artificial gravity, Jinto's body could not discern any change on account of attitude control. His only indication of the ship's movement was his view of the stars on the screen. Craning his neck, Jinto spotted Delktou in the distance. *So tiny!*

"Attitude control complete."

"Daisielle!" Lexshu called for the lift anchor.

Water began to flow into the antimatter annihilation engines (Flisesia), absorbing the antiprotons. Matter and antimatter collided, annihilating each other, leaving only enormous energy. The excess water sucked up the energy, and shot out into the vacuum of space, propelling the ship with enormous recoil.

"Bored yet?" Lexshu politely inquired.

"Not at all," Jinto answered without having to lie.

"Do you have any questions?"

"Yes." Jinto thought for a moment, managing to concoct a safe question. "Now, I was under the impression that Lekle Saryush was the senior gunnery officer, but he seems to be in charge of steering, too. Isn't the Tlakia — the navigator?"

"Yes. In Dath, or normal space, steering is included in the Tlakia job description. On a Resii, battle and navigation are completely interrelated."

"I see." He paused. "I have another question."

"Okay. Shoot."

"I thought a clerk was responsible for the ship's office work, but he seems to be employed on the Gahorl."

"True. He is responsible for ensuring that the gravity is correct and that the atmosphere within the ship is stable. The Wiigt, or clerk, is only on the Gahorl when we enter or leave port, or when we do battle, so he attends to most of his duties in the clerk's office."

Jinto cocked his head. "What exactly does he *do* in there?"

She smiled. "Ah, yes. A Lonyu's destiny! You should ask Diesh directly."

Hecto-Commander Lexshu answered Jinto's questions to the best of her ability, and Jinto deemed her to be a kind woman. He did feel she regarded him as a child, but he didn't mind.

Eventually, the Lowas Reilia broadcast a report. "Sord passage in three minutes."

"But we're right in the middle of a conversation!" The captain looked at Jinto. "Sorry, kiddo. Create Flasath!"

"Flasatia is operational," said Lowas Skem Gumrua as he switched on the engine that created a protective space-time bubble around the ship.

The gate to Vorash, dead ahead, was the second form of a Yuanon: a phosphorescent, spherical singularity space, approximately one Sedarjh in diameter. The Abh called it a Sord Gulark or more simply, a Sord. The Abh referred to the first form of Yuanon—the kind that powered ships like the *Leif Erickson*—as Sord Loeza.

"Sord passage in one minute."

"Begin countdown at thirty seconds," the Sarerl ordered.

"Roger."

By the time the countdown began, the grayish light of the Sord blanketed the space in front of the ship.

"Five. Four. Three. Two. One. Passage."

As they passed through the Sord, Jinto noticed only the distinct *lack* of sensation. It was as peaceful as being underwater in an ash-colored sea.

The secret to traveling faster than the speed of light was Fath, an alternate universe with different laws of physics than normal space.

Fath, or Plane Space, was an aptly named universe comprising only *two* spatial dimensions and one time dimension. Wrapped in Flasath, the Abh's interstellar spaceships exited regular time and space and entered the separate universe of Fath. The Flasath, or space-time bubble, was a slice of normal space that encased the ship, enabling it to exist in two dimensions.

Safe in their alternate universe, they wouldn't even know if calamity struck normal space. Jinto shuddered at the thought.

"Estimate position," the Sarerl ordered, then turned to Jinto. "We don't know our current position."

"Why not?"

"Once we've shifted from Dath to Fath, we can only know our position based on probability theory."

Jinto thought he recalled hearing that phrase in an introductory lecture on the rudiments of Plane Space technology (Faz Fathoth).

"I thought that was mostly all talk."

"It is. Pretty much," she assented. "If normal space were a box, we would travel in a straight line across its surface. Flying through Dath is like cutting through the inside of the box. Unfortunately, Dath is not a straight line. It's twisted and contorted like a really gnarled tree branch. Our navigational equipment cannot read its shape, so we can only guess where we are in here, based on where we would be on the surface of the box."

She sighed. "The inside of a Sord is like the inside of a spiral seashell. Points on the outside of a Sord correspond to locations inside the shell, but it's not precise. Thus, we can only approximate our position in Fath, based on the corresponding normal space location."

"Position confirmation complete," reported the navigator. "Right bank—one hundred seven point ninety-two from terminus."

"Commence Noktaf at two hundred eighty degrees." Again, the captain made sure Jinto understood. "You know about Noktaf and Skobrotaf?"

To an outside observer, a Flasath looked like a single rotating particle. Noktaf and Skobrotaf described the direction of a Flasath's revolution. Every Sazoirl needed to know that in order to enroll.

"Yes," Jinto said, although numerical representations of Noktaf and Skobrotaf still boggled him.

Jinto remembered learning that a Flasath in Fath was like a ball spinning on the floor. If its axis of rotation was perpendicular to the floor, then it would remain stationary, but if the ball rotated around an axis parallel to the floor, then it would roll. A rolling ball was Noktaf, and a stationary ball was Skobrotaf.

Now, the Flasath's rotational speed was constant, so any adjustments to travel speed had to come from adjusting the angle of the axis of rotation.

"From this point forward, navigation is the Rilbiga's job," whispered Lexshu, pointing to Reilia. She grew louder. "Destination: Sord Sufagnaum. Calculate course."

On the display screen, the Sord resembled a warped and twisted spiral. Almost immediately after Lexshu's order, a dotted blue line appeared, charting a course for the ship.

Reilia looked to the Sarerl. "Calculation complete."

"Acknowledged. I'll leave it up to you, Reilia, to follow the course."

"Roger, Sarerl. I'll take care of it."

The blue blob of light representing the ship began to move toward the dotted line. Other blips of light appeared on the screen—probably other ships approaching Dreuhynu Vorlak. Once the blue blip reached the dotted blue line, it latched onto it like a skier to a tow rope.

"We've set course, Sarerl," announced Reilia.

Putting away her Kiseg, the Hecto-Commander announced, "Excellent. Complete crew function fulfilled. Switch to number one duty condition."

Only three of the officers on the bridge remained seated. Everyone else stood, saluted the captain, then left.

Unsure what to do, Jinto fidgeted in his seat.

The captain returned to her chair. "Lonyu, I don't want you to get bored on your first experience. From this point forward, these Lodair just monitor the equipment for malfunctions. Not terribly exciting, so I'll have someone show you to your room."

"If it's all right," Jinto said, not wanting to impose, "I'd like to stay and talk to you for a little while."

"Of course, Lonyu. Between you and me, I find this part quite tedious anyway. What did you want to talk about?"

"Are you familiar with the history of Dreujhe Haider?"

"Yes. The conquest of the Count Hyde's nation is common knowledge."

Strange, Jinto thought. *The way Lexshu said "conquest" did not connote "invasion" at all.*

"So, it shouldn't surprise you that I have no clue how to act like a Sif."

"Really?" Apparently, it wasn't as obvious as Jinto originally thought.

"Yes. I'm very much out of my element."

She frowned. "You haven't socialized with the Dreujhe Vorlak?"

"No." The Count Vorash had not initiated any relationship with the next Hyde Count, and Jinto didn't want to go out of his way to visit the count's orbital mansion (Garish). "I've never been invited."

"Essentially, what you're saying is that you don't know how to treat us?"

"Yes." Jinto nodded. "I don't even know whether it's weird for me to ask you these kinds of questions."

"No, no." Lexshu smiled. "It's a rare opportunity for a Lef to teach a Voda how to act."

He sighed. "So my behavior *is* strange, then."

"Voda are usually more arrogant," said the Hecto-Commander. "However, that doesn't exactly win them any friends."

"So, you're saying I'm not *that* weird."

Lexshu put a finger to her pursed lips. "Eccentric, maybe. But not in a bad way."

"Ha ha ha . . ." Jinto laughed and melted into his seat. He shook his head.

It only took Lexshu a moment of silence to understand Jinto's disappointment. "You *do* know your social standing is higher than mine, right?" she asked.

"Really? I kept thinking you're more respectful than you ought to be."

"Interesting." The captain cocked an eyebrow, the same way a person might look at a monkey wearing underpants on its head.

Jinto said, "I understand Sune, but have no clue about the social status of non-royalty. I've tried to investigate, but everything I found only made me more confused. I thought it was commonplace for a noble to work under Lef in the Frybar."

"Yes, it's very common."

"So, then, isn't that equivalent to my having no social status?"

"In relationships between people who belong to different organizations, Imperial court rank is what counts," Lexshu explained. "As Sarerl, I am the Larosh on this ship. That's pretty good standing for Lef, but it doesn't hold a candle to Jarluk Dreu."

"And that's not confusing to anybody else?" Jinto wondered.

"Why would it be?"

"If a subordinate rates higher socially than the superior officer, doesn't that make it hard to give him orders?"

The Hecto-Commander laughed lightly. "Only if they belong to different organizations. In the military, this is what counts," she said, pointing to the rank insignia on her right upper arm, the same way Lafiel had earlier. Maybe it was a common gesture among officers in the Labule. "If Your Excellency were under my command as a Lodair Sazoirl, I'd bust your chops just like anyone else."

"It's all very confusing." Jinto sighed. "Is it like age?"

"What do you mean?" she asked.

Jinto explained that on Delktou, respect increased proportionally to age. They called it "the order of old and young."

Even if a young person were in charge of an older person at work, as soon as they left the office, they swapped standing. This would likely confuse the hell out of the Abh, who had no discernible difference in age.

"Maybe so," Lexshu agreed moderately. "We're hardly ever conscious of age."

"Right. I still don't get why a person is considered superior just because he's born into a high-ranking family."

As soon as he'd said it, Jinto realized he'd criticized one of the pillars of the Frybar society. He expected the Sarerl to be shaken, but his words effected no change in her face.

Reading Abh minds, Jinto decided, *is borderline impossible.*

"Ah, yes," the captain said. "A noble is the progeny of superior people. A Sif will inherit a Jhedirl built by superior people. Of course we expect Imperial nobles to be superior, too. And thus we respect them."

"The best people in the world could raise a slug, and it would always be a slug."

She smiled. "Sure, there are those rare occasions where children of heroes turn out to be total duds, but for the most part, children of excellent people tend to retain many qualities of their forebears' excellence. And they often demonstrate it in a unique way."

"Okay." Jinto nodded, thinking about his own upbringing. Even if his father was a "superior" person, he certainly hadn't raised Jinto.

"Has this been helpful?"

"Yes, thank you." Although he couldn't whole-heartedly approve of the Abh social system, she had done a good job explaining it.

"In that case, I'll have someone guide you to your room—the Bene who came to meet you at the Bidaut."

Of course she means Lafiel. Jinto brightened. "She's nobility, too, right?"

Lexshu's eyes widened. "You really don't you know who she is?"

"No. Um . . ." Jinto searched his brain. "Should I?"

"I guess it's only natural, given Your Excellency's eccentric way of life." The captain smiled and set her Kreuno to the communications function. "Bene Lodair Abriel to the bridge at once."

"Abriel?" It was the same as the Glaharerl Rue Byrer that had invaded the Hyde star system. *He* was a member of the Imperial family (Fasanzoerl); it was the name of the Imperial house (Ruejhe). "Which Abriel is she?"

"She's a Lartei Kryb."

"So . . ."

"Yes." A wicked little smile spread across her lovely face. "Bene Lodair Abriel is the granddaughter of Spunej Ramaj Erumita."

Jinto gaped. *Lafiel is a princess!*

The Frybar relied heavily on its military, so it was expected that the Spunej would have experience in the Star Force. However, the governance of the Humankind Empire of Abh (Frybar Gloer Gor Bari) was not a military dictatorship; there were also hereditary and dispositional prerequisites for taking the royal throne (Skemsoraj).

However, the Abh were smart enough to know that automatically making the highest-ranking military official the Spunej would be problematic; military dictatorships had met with disastrous results throughout the entire history of humankind. Fearing the dissolution of the Frybar, the Abh instituted a method for the inheritance of the throne (Kilugraj) of the Frybar Gloer Gor Bari that took disposition into account in addition to heredity.

Basically, the Fasanzoerl comprised eight royal families (Lartei). They were descendants of Dunei, the Founding Emperor (Skurleteria), or his siblings. Thus, they all had the family name, or Fiith, of Abriel.

Each emperor came from one of eight royal families: Lartei Skirh, Nei Lamral; Lartei Irik, Nei Duswiel; Lartei Lasiser, Nei Lomryulal; Lartei Weskor, Nei Dueil; Lartei

Barker, Nei Lamsar; Lartei Balgzeder, Nei Dubuzel; Lartei Shulgzeder, Nei Duasek; and Lartei Kryb, Nei Debrusc.

The expectations placed the children of the Eight Royal Houses (Ga Lartei) were extremely high—military service was required of them. Children who became administrators and doctors were considered disappointments!

Fasanzoerl were granted the privilege of entering a military university (Voskura) after only two years of military service (Slymekoth), instead of the four years required of non-royal applicants. After a year and a half, they earned the rank, or Renyu, of a Lowas. From that point on, they advanced at the same speed as other Voskura graduates.

Starting from line wing officer, there were twelve steps up the ladder to Lodair Gariar. Once Fasanzoerl reached the rank of Imperial Admiral (Rue Spen), they were appointed as Imperial Fleet Commander-in-Chief. Most of the time this was an honorary title with no responsibilities attached. However, it did indicate that the person was the next in line to become the Emperor.

Once a new Glaharerl Rue Byrer was chosen, the rest of the Fasanzoerl customarily requested reassignment into the first reserve. Some Fasanzoerl gave up trying to become Emperor and retired from the military, choosing to inherit their throne or become a lifelong Fasanzoerl with their Sune. Descendants of lifetime Fasanzoerl took the Fiith "Baus" to indicate that they inherited Jhedirl from the Ruejhe, but they were only Imperial nobles. Imperial nobles were not allowed to use the name Abriel.

Usually, the Commander-in-Chief held his position until the appearance of the next Rue Spen, at which time he resigned to allow the latter's ascension to the throne.

When Emperors resigned, they often had as much as a hundred years of life left. Thus, they were not permitted to *truly* retire. Instead, ex-Emperors took on the honorary title of "Your Grace" (Nisoth) in the Former Emperor's Congress (known as Luzei Fanigalak).

The Luzei Fanigalak presided over the promotions of Fasanzoerl Lodair and was, in practice, more severely critical than the military. Children of the Ga Lartei had forty years to struggle their way through the Luzei Fanigalak's interviews and performance reviews.

While he waited for the Pilot trainee to arrive, Jinto perused the who's who of Imperial persons (Rue Lalasa) on his Kreuno. Abriel Nei Debrusc, Viscount of Parhynu Lafiel, he found, was the first princess (Lartnei Kasna) born of Larth Kryb Debeus.

It was like a surprise attack.

Jinto had always expected to meet royalty, just not the way he'd met Lafiel. He expected to come across them at dinner parties, social functions, or ceremonies. But this . . .

There he was, just a step behind an extremely close blood-relative of the monarch of the Frybar, the ruler who governed nine hundred billion subjects.

Jinto began to fear that his behavior inside the shuttle had been improper.

How can I clear this up? he wondered.

Looking around for inspiration, Jinto was surprised to see that the interior of the Wikreurl was covered in murals of grassy fields beneath blue skies with fluffy, white clouds. Although it should have had a soothing effect, Jinto felt no assurance.

"What's wrong, Jinto?" Lafiel asked. "Why are you so quiet all of a sudden? And . . . why are you now walking behind me?"

"Well, Feia Ruer . . ." Jinto began, calling her by the Abh title—Her Highness the Imperial Princess.

Lafiel stopped dead in her tracks and turned around. Her glare was sharp enough to make any honest man pray for death. Despite the fact that rage colored her face and small fires seemed to be burning in her pupils, Lafiel spoke more coldly than ever. "I'm not Ruene. My grandmother is Spunej, but my father is only a Larth."

"I'm very sorry, Feia Lartneir," Jinto responded, bowing, perhaps excessively. *Man. Is it that big a deal to mix up her Traiga?*

Having corrected him, Lafiel turned away and began to walk quickly down the hall. Jinto hustled after her.

She spoke, marching straight ahead. "Since I'm Spunej Erumita's granddaughter, you could call me Rue Bogne. That's not very formal, though, so nobody does that. It came as a shock to me when I discovered I was the Empress' granddaughter. Feia Rue Bogne. That sounds terrible."

"Yeah—I mean, yes, Feia."

"With my father as guardian, I inherited the Traiga and the Ribeun of Viscount of Parhynu from Spunej Erumita. So, you could also call me Feia Borl Paryun. Or, as most people on the ship do, you could call me Bene Lodair Abriel," Lafiel spouted. She hadn't stopped to breathe in quite some time.

Unable to get a word in edgewise, Jinto just struggled to keep up with her.

"However, I told you to call me Lafiel!"

"Oh, I'm sorry," Jinto said. "I get it. Your friends call you Lafiel."

"No," Lafiel answered curtly. "Only my father, my grandmother, and my aunt address me without a Traiga. Just them, and the direct descendants of the former emperors. That's it. My friends call me Feia Lartneir or Feia. My relatives mostly call me Feia Lafiel."

As he mulled this over, Jinto's legs involuntarily stopped moving. Realizing that she had granted him a monumental honor without him even knowing it, Jinto was dumbstruck. "Then why would I call you Lafiel, especially when we just met?"

"My grandmother is the Spunej. Everybody already knows my name and calls me Feia Lartneir without even asking. When I met you, it was the first time anybody'd ever asked me my name. Even my very intimate companions call me Feia. That's how it's been since I was born, so I never really took notice of it, until at the Kenru I noticed all the other students just called each other by name without Traiga. I was . . . only the slightest bit . . . jealous."

"I'm sorry." Jinto was truly appalled by his own abuse of her trust and goodwill.

"There's no need to apologize," Lafiel said, stinging Jinto with coldness. "I know you didn't say Feia Ruer out of spite. Now, I wasn't brought up to tolerate rude names, but I'll accept any one of my proper titles. You may call me Feia Lartneir or Feia Borl Paryun, whichever suits you, Lonyu Jarluk Dreu."

"What's wrong with 'Lafiel'?" he asked.

"Let me make this clear. It's not that I really *want* to be called Lafiel. It's just that when you asked my name, I wasn't thinking about which Traiga to call myself."

Jinto hid a smile. *If she wants to be Spunej, she'll have to get better at lying.*

"Please, I'd like to call you Lafiel, if that's okay."

She finally turned around and looked at Jinto. "I won't force you, Lonyu."

"You're not forcing—"

"I wouldn't even mind Feia Rue Bogne."

"For crying out loud!" Jinto hollered. "Can you ever forgive me, Lafiel?"

For a minute, Lafiel said nothing. She just stared at Jinto. Then, her lips trembled slightly, and the formerly angry Lartnei began to snicker. Suddenly, like water through a burst dam, laughter gushed out.

Jinto breathed a big sigh of relief, knowing they were probably back on friendly terms.

"You really didn't know I was an Abriel?" Lafiel asked once she got herself together.

He shrugged. "Nope. No clue."

"Even when you saw these ears?" She pulled back her hair, revealing pointy ears, similar to those of the Abriel Glaharerl who had invaded the Hyde star system several years before. "These are Abriel ears—the Wariit of our family."

"I couldn't see them underneath all that hair," Jinto justified.

"I suppose I do have pretty small ears for an Abriel," she stated somewhat dejectedly.

"Regardless," Jinto continued, "it's questionable whether I would have noticed even if I'd seen your ears. As a non-native Abh, I am not familiar with Wariit."

Lafiel considered this. Wariit were the specific physical characteristics shared by families, such as ear and nose shape, eye and skin color, eyebrow bushiness, etc. The Abh were pretty fanatical about maintaining a similar appearance to their families, regardless of their rank or social status.

Nui Abliarsar, the Abriel ears, was the most famous of Wariit. Until that moment, however, Jinto forgot such a thing even existed. He started walking down the hall, shaking his head.

Lafiel fell in beside him. "You're funny."

Shrugging, Jinto laughed nervously. "Can I tell you something . . . ? About what you just said?"

"What did I just say?"

"The memories of your Kenru—you said that when the other kids were with you, they couldn't seem to relax."

Nodding, Lafiel encouraged him to go on.

"I think I had a similar experience." Jinto smiled, slightly embarrassed. "To a lesser degree."

"How so?"

"Well, I was the only nobleman in school."

"Oh, I see."

Preparing for assimilation into the Abh culture, most students at the Abh language and culture school harbored dreams of being conferred Lef or, for the super-lucky, Imperial nobility. Needless to say, they were enormously envious to hear that there was a lander among them who was guaranteed a Sune status.

Nobody knew how to treat a Sif. Some teased and tormented Jinto, finding him in the back of the classroom, just beyond the teachers' vision. Other kids were overly respectful, to the point of mutual discomfort.

"It's okay that they didn't know how to act around me—I didn't even know how *I* should act."

"In my case, Kenyu knew how to treat Fasanzoerl. I just didn't care for it. You know, it was probably harder for you. I will never be teased."

Jinto couldn't help thinking that maybe she *wanted* someone to tease her, just to escape the isolation. But he wasn't about to go there. "It's strange. I never did anything to provoke it. I just had too many enemies, including the teachers."

Lafiel nodded.

"Luckily, I learned an essential survival skill at any early age."

"Which was?" Lafiel asked with unfeigned interest.

"Hiding my social standing."

Lafiel tilted her head. "Is that even possible?"

"Well, I'm not as famous as Feia Lartneir, but . . ." After a moment, Jinto shook his head. "No. It didn't work at all. Even if I managed to fool somebody, there was always a blabbermouth around."

"What did you do?" she asked.

"I went to the city, where I became friends with Sos who have no relationship at all to the Frybar."

"Sounds like you went to an awful lot of trouble."

As they were about to pass in the hallway, two Sash stopped and saluted. Lafiel returned the salute without stopping.

"Hey," Jinto half-whispered. "Should I salute, too?"

"Just nod."

Taking the Sash by surprise, Jinto turned and nodded to them. They quickly saluted a second time.

"Don't confuse them, Jinto," Lafiel rebuked him playfully.

"Got it." He sighed, but needn't have worried; his next interaction with Sash was as smooth as an eggshell.

Stopping in front of a door with a giant picture of a sunflower on it, Lafiel turned to Jinto. "These are your quarters."

"What's the deal with these pictures?" Jinto stared at the door. "What do they mean?"

"They're for decoration. They don't *mean* anything," said Lafiel. "Makes the Wikreurl more pleasant, don't you think?"

"It seems really out of place," Jinto grumbled. "I mean, isn't there a design more suitable for a spaceship?"

"Like what?"

"I don't know . . . something intergalactic. Stars or galaxies or something."

"Who would ever paint something that boring?"

Taken aback, Jinto said he thought the Abh loved space.

"We do. Space is our home. But stars are so commonplace. If you want stars, look out the window." She shrugged.

"That's true, I guess."

"Besides, these paintings are soothing to the Nahen-native Sash."

"I see." Jinto eyeballed the sunflower. "But what do you Abh think?"

"How many times do I have to remind you that *you're* Abh, too?"

"Not by birth. I am not up to speed on the proper reaction to plants." He grinned.

"It should be no different from that of landers, I would think." Lafiel frowned. "We're the descendants of Gloe who originated from Earth, you know."

"But you've probably never seen a real sunflower," Jinto guessed.

"Don't be silly. We had a flower garden at home. There are botanical gardens all over the place on Lakfakalle."

"Oh." Jinto turned around and pointed to the meadow mural behind them. "What about that?"

The wall depicted a lush lea and a variety of large fauna grazing on the knee-high grass. Cherry blossoms swirled through the sky, near the tops of scattered pine and birch trees.

"I've definitely never seen anything like that," Lafiel said after a moment.

"How does it look to you?"

A moment passed before Lafiel answered. "It looks like a scene in a dream."

"Because it's surreal?"

"No," Lafiel thought aloud, tilting her head. "I know it does exist, and that we supposedly came from it. It's like a myth."

"So this is the Abh's old home planet?"

"Yes. Now Kesath," she said, waving her hands in a circle to indicate space in its entirety, "where we're proud to be the only Kesateudo, is our home."

"Even landers are the descendants of space travelers," Jinto pointed out.

"There's a big difference. The ancestors of landers only passed through space. We *live* here."

"Good point," said Jinto, although he wasn't sure if it was.

"How does this look to you, Jinto?" Lafiel asked. "Are you as bored with this as we are looking at stars? And by 'we,' I meant native-born Abh."

"No, I'm not bored. There's hardly any scenery like this where I grew up. My old home's ecosystem was different from other land worlds', so I guess this isn't far enough from reality to be called fantastical. I mean, to the eyes of a botanist, this would probably be totally ridiculous, but . . . Hey, are you going to show me how to open this door, or what?"

Lafiel pouted. "You were the one who wanted to talk about the sunflowers."

"Well, it was interesting."

"Yes, it's the first time I've ever really examined that picture."

Lafiel, Jinto thought, *has a generally agreeable disposition.* He smiled and nodded toward the door.

"Just use your Kreuno; its electromagnetic waveform is already registered."

"Okay." Jinto touched the red stone on the display of his Kreuno. The door opened. "Whoa," he said as he peered in.

"Are you dissatisfied?"

"Far from it! I certainly didn't expect to find it in such an orderly condition."

The room was not large, and the bed took up most of the space. There was a table, a chair, and another smaller door. The Guraw Mongarl, the banner of the Hyde nation, hung on the wall next to the bed.

It depicted a red Lezwan in a field of green. The creature resembled a bird but was actually a species of hair-covered fish native to Martine's saltwater seas. Although the Lezwan was an undeniably stupid animal, it looked quite majestic with its furry fins spread out.

Indicating a set of shelves opposite the bed, Lafiel said, "Your luggage will fit there. If you want to clean up, go through that little door."

Jinto peeked through the door. Just as he suspected, it contained a washroom, complete with a shower. "This is great. Is this a passenger bedroom?"

"This is a Resii," she said, as if it were an absurd question. "It's a standard officer's room."

"Officer's room? I didn't take somebody else's spot, did I?"

"There's plenty of room for everybody. On Wikreurl the size of a Resii, there's always plenty of living space, because you never know if more crew members might come aboard. I'm an extra crew member, you know."

Jinto couldn't stop staring at the banner. "Where did that thing come from?"

"We made it."

"Just for me?"

"Why would we make it for anyone else?"

But why would you bother for me?

Answering Lafiel's question with a shrug of his shoulders, Jinto determined that he was indifferent to the hastily designed crest (called an Ajh). Though many people were attached to their coat of arms, Jinto had forgotten his family even had one until that day.

Jinto sat on the soft bed and predicted very sound sleep in his future. "So, what should I do now?"

"Right." Lafiel looked at the time display on her Kreuno. "You have two hours until dinner. You'll probably be invited to the Sarerl's table. I'll come get you when it's time. Until then, just sit tight."

"That seems like a big pain in the butt for you. Just call me on the Luode; I'm sure I can find it myself."

"Bad idea," Lafiel said. "Seriously. I've been instructed to give you a tour tomorrow, but until then, don't walk around by yourself. The ship's interior guide maps are tricky; I can't even count how many civilians and new recruits have withered away in remote corners of ships since the Labule was founded."

"What about you? You ever get lost?" Jinto probed evilly.

"That's a rather rude question," she said.

"That sounds like a yes."

"Shut up," Lafiel snapped. "Do you need anything else from me?"

"Nope. Nothing, thanks. I'll just be here, quietly imagining you as a new recruit, wandering aimlessly. Hopelessly lost in—"

"In two hours, then." She was *not* amused.

"Yes, two hours."

Turning on her heels, Lafiel bolted.

Alone, Jinto decided it'd be nice to take a hot bath. As he undressed, he was surprised to find that he was perfectly calm. All the stress he'd felt prior to boarding the ship had melted somewhere along the way.

6 Emergency (Lesliamroth)

Hecto-Commander Lexshu Wef-Robell Plakia awoke a split-second before the hologram of Lowas Reilia appeared beside her bed.

"Sarerl," Lowas Reilia addressed the captain.

"What is it?"

"Please come to the Gahorl at once," he grimly requested. "We've detected unknown Flasath."

"I'm on my way." Waving her hand to cut off the Luode, she sprang out of bed. Without even turning on a light, she pulled on her Serlin, straightened her hair, and put on her winged tiara. On her way out the door, she grabbed her Kutaroev and Greu, then walked quickly toward the bridge.

Inside the tube, she deftly wrapped the Kutaroev around her hips and hung the Greu from it.

By the time she arrived at the bridge, Lexshu was completely and formally attired.

"Report, Reilia!" Lexshu shouted as she ran onto the bridge.

"Direction: seventy-eight degrees ahead. Distance: fifteen hundred thirty-nine point one seven Kedlairl. Course:

eighteen degrees ahead. That's the direction of Loebehynu Sufagnaum," Lowas Reilia spat out in one breath while jumping out of the captain's seat, where he had sat while the Bomowas slept.

Lexshu didn't sit down. "That's our next port of call, isn't it? Safugnoff?"

"Yes." Reilia assented. "At current speeds, we'll arrive first."

"What's its scale?"

"One hundred twenty confirmed Flasath, with a total mass of about ninety Zesabo. That's comparable to four Jadbyr."

Lexshu stared at the map of Plane Space (called a Ja Flasath) on the floor.

There were a number of Sord, winding black coils, lurking in the vicinity of the ship, which appeared as a blinking blue dot.

Due to their constant energy emissions, Sord and solar winds repelled each other. This, in conjunction with the gate's relatively small mass in normal space, meant that they were generally located on the outskirts of star systems.

However, Sord on the other side of the event horizon took in more energy than they gave off. In these cases, for the majority of Sord, the energy flowed from Fath to Dath. The Abh name for these special eruptive Sord was Kiigaf.

Kiigaf were like volcanoes that continuously spewed space-time particles (Supflasath) from Plane Space into Dath. When they went from Plane Space to normal space, Supflasath were reduced to four-dimensional space-time particles about the size of an electron.

Flasath absorbed Supflasath, reacted with them, and then ejected a much greater quantity of Supflasath. The byproduct of these reactions was an enormous amount of energy, which was the fuel that propelled the first Yuanon-powered ships.

Flasath also emitted mass waves (Sesuwas) that could be detected from very far away. The unidentified objects on the *Gosroth's* radar were undeniably Flasath.

The Sarerl knew something was amiss. She would have known in advance if allies were moving a fleet of that size; an unexpected movement of this magnitude indicated an emergency situation.

She didn't even want to think what it meant if these ships weren't allies.

It would be much easier if we could just ask them what's going on, Lexshu thought.

Unfortunately, the laws of physics prohibited that kind of communication in Fath. The frequencies and wavelengths of Sesuwas were fixed in Plane Space. Consequently, they overlapped and created unavoidable interference.

Sadly, sending Supflasath was the only effective means of communication between Flasath. However, this space-time bubble's (Drosh Flacteder) transmission speed was unbearably slow and only worked over very short distances.

"From which Sord did they come?"

"Rinjer Lesheikuryua is calculating that right now," Reilia replied.

After a tense moment of number crunching, Rilbiga Lesheikuryua reported, "I've narrowed it down to forty-seven possible Sord of entry. Beyond that, it's impossible."

"Among those, which Sord are in use?" asked Lexshu.

"They've all been left in the Sord Loeza state," Lesheikuryua said, shaking his head.

"What about Sord that exist within one lightyear of inhabited planets?"

It took a moment for Lesheikuryua to sort through the old data from the scout fleet (named the Byr Ragrlot) on his computer crystal. "There is none."

"Within five lightyears?"

"Uh . . . just one."

"Where?"

"Planet Vascotton IV, in the Vascotton star system. Four point one lightyears from Sord Kikotosokunbina Keik. It belongs to the United Mankind!"

"Figures," Reilia chimed in.

The Abh race originated from a ship full of arms merchants who roamed through space aboard the colony ship *Abriel*—of course, this was the origin of the Lueje surname—carrying eight Sord Loeza in its hold.

Although they technically considered themselves to be merchants, they were self-sufficient and, within the confines of their ship, produced everything they needed to survive. Thus, information was the primary currency in Abh trades.

They dealt in histories, technologies, scientific reports, works of art—pretty much anything produced by people that revealed anything about their culture. There were lightyears of nothingness between human societies, and the *Abriel* was the only thin thread connecting these societies. Consequently, people were always excited to find something to relate to in a distant corner of the universe and were happy to pay exorbitant sums for it.

After indicating what kind of services they could provide, the Abh fixed a price. Unusual merchants, the Abh detested haggling, and whenever their negotiations broke down, they simply left the star system.

If they felt cheated, the Abh only absconded after exacting whatever revenge they deemed appropriate. Often, they would later discover that it was merely a tragic misunderstanding. It was never practical to backtrack multiple lightyears just to apologize.

As a result of their somewhat rash behavior, the Abh became infamous, with a reputation for being arrogant and reckless. This reputation only ballooned after the founding of the Frybar.

After many years of gathering and selling the essence of human society, the Abh became intergalactic recluses, intent on developing Plane Space technology.

It took fifty years, but as the first to discover it, the Abh decided they would be the *only* ones to use it.

They reasoned that, spread so far apart, human worlds had never even considered the prospect of interstellar war. However, Fath technology (and faster-than-light travel) made it feasible. Although the Abh couldn't think of a reason why the star systems couldn't coexist peacefully, they also knew that humans were unparalleled at concocting reasons to kill each other. Now that the capability existed for people to wage intergalactic wars, the Abh didn't want to let them take advantage of it. Thus, they decided to monopolize the new technology.

At the time Skurleteria Dokunei declared the Frybar's independence, there were, according to statisticians, 202,904 Abh. Abh demographers estimated the total human population to be more than a hundred billion.

The Abh knew that, eventually, someone else would unlock the secrets of Plane Space technology. In order to prevent others from using it, the Abh decided to unify all of humankind and control the rate of discovery by force.

Given those numbers, it was not hard to see how they came to have a reputation for arrogance.

One setback for the Abh was that they weren't actually the first humans to enter Fath; earlier, a settlement in the Sumei star system also discovered Plane Space (purely by accident). The Sumei were more than happy to sell the secret to anyone who could afford it.

This continued for some time, while the blissfully unaware Abh began their conquest of the inhabitable universe. They already controlled five star systems by the time they noticed someone else had beaten them into Fath. Needless to say, they were not pleased.

Abh theory dictated that governance of the universe should be kept simple; everybody should follow the same constitution. According to Abh law, they were the only race "burdened" with space travel, which didn't appeal to landers anyway. If landers would just stick to their planets and find happiness there, then everyone would get along just fine.

Unfortunately for the Abh, other interstellar nations disagreed with the Frybar.

The Abh respected vested rights, so they did not attempt to colonize any nations that purchased the Sumei technology. However, as soon as they learned of a Nahen that didn't know about Plane Space technology (what the Abh called Faz Fathoth), they invaded without hesitation.

Just as the Abh feared, interstellar nations found millions of ways to disagree, nobody trusted anybody else, conflicts escalated, and swords crossed.

The fates of entire nations rested on these battles, and the Abh just watched. The Abh didn't want to get involved in these disputes, but sometimes it was unavoidable.

Forced to resort to war, the Abh rose (or perhaps sank) to a whole new level of ruthlessness. Once they started to fight, they did not stop until they had stolen the enemy's means of interstellar travel, decimated their weapons, and assimilated any remaining citizens into the Frybar.

The Abh incurred some losses during their campaign; there were the remains of two Spunej and seven Kilugia, among others, scattered throughout space. Mostly, though, the Abh victory song "Frybar Gloer Gor Bari" rang loud and clear throughout the galaxy.

Of course, the other interstellar nations viewed the Frybar as a threat, so they tried to keep their distance. After a series of divisions, mergers, and conquests, there were four interstellar nations (other than the Abh). They were the United Mankind, the Hania Federation, the Republic of Greater Alcont, and the People's Sovereign Union of Star Systems. These nations all adopted democratic governments.

When Fath technology was new, the nascent governments met in United Mankind's Nova Sicily star system. Able to put aside their differences, they concocted and adhered to a peace treaty that was *nearly* all-inclusive; the Frybar was excluded from the treaty.

That treaty, known as the Nova Sicily Treaty, established a union called the Nova Sicily Treaty Organization Nations. For short, the people called it The Democratic Nations, or just the D.N. The Frybar called them Bruvoth Gos Syuyn for the Four Nations Alliance.

For twelve years, the treaty fulfilled its primary purpose, preventing war between the nations and protecting them from the Frybar. The D.N. had strength in numbers; United Mankind, the largest of the nations, counted over six hundred billion citizens, and the combined population of the four nations was close to one point one trillion.

The Frybar honored the treaty, but continued to conquer any nations who weren't involved with it. For some time, there were no major confrontations.

The Nova Sicily Treaty Organization Nations harbored secret resentment about the Empire's domination. Over the years, there were no overt hostilities, but the rift between the groups continued to grow, quite profoundly. The tension continued to escalate, and recent communications indicated the conflict was near its boiling point.

The straw that broke the camel's back, so to speak, was the Frybar invasion of the Hyde star system.

The Abh believed that the D. N. shouldn't have waited seven years to do something about it. The D.N. *had* filed a Declaration of Protest, which was its standard procedure against an Abh conquest.

It wasn't until six years after the subjugation of the Hyde star system that the Democratic Nations decided it was actually an unforgivable transgression.

"Hmm," Lexshu assessed. "It looks like the Bruvoth Gos Syuyn is itching for a battle. Their demands are completely unreasonable; we cannot make Dreuhynu Haider independent, nor can we allow them unrestricted passage through Frybar territories. They know the Empire could never agree to that."

"So?" Reilia raised one eyebrow.

"Don't you see? It's just an excuse. They've had something up their sleeves the whole time. And now they're ready to put the cards on the table."

"Makes sense. They've been been plotting for ages."

In order to enact their plan, the United Mankind had to collect scattered Sord Loeza and open them to see whether they corresponded to useful locations on the Fath side.

They must have sorted through myriads of useless Sord before finding one that *didn't* lead them straight into Abh territory. Once they found an appropriate Sord, they still had to transport it close to an inhabited planet by way of normal space.

They had to wait for the Sord to close before transporting it. Left in a low energy state, a Sord Gulark would become a Sord Loeza. But that took twelve years!

"They've probably been at work at least since Dreuhynu Haider was founded," Reilia added.

"Dreuhynu Haider is not the big issue. I'll bet these plans predate the Nova Sicily Treaty," Lexshu said.

Reilia scratched his chin. "Then why would they tell such an obvious lie?"

Lexshu sighed. "It's not for our sake, but theirs. They are only fooling themselves."

"I don't get it."

The captain sighed. "Well, I'm no expert in their psychology, but maybe they'd like to believe that they're allies of righteousness. That their battle is justified."

"Ah, very honorable. So *we're* the bad guys?" Reilia kind of liked this idea.

"Don't you know?" Lexshu asked, amused. "We're the worst! Bandits, butchers, et cetera. Just take a look in a United Mankind history book—you'll see all the 'atrocities' we've committed."

"Change in the enemy Flasath group!" the Drokia interjected. Nobody bothered to correct the young Fektodai for his assumptive identification of the Flasath as "the enemy."

Gazing at the unidentified Flasath group, Lexshu waited for the communications officer to continue.

"It split into ten. And now they've changed course toward us. Judging from their mass, these appear to be assault-class warship Flasath."

The maximum speed of a Flasath was proportional to its mass. Technological efficiency improvements were not effective, so a Flasath could only be as fast as it was light. Thus, battleships and transport ships were slower than patrol ships. Assault ships, however, were a different story. It was disarmingly clear the group of Flasath that separated intended to seize the *Gosroth*.

"When will our 'friends' enter Hoksath range?"

The Drokia said, "At 21:15, internal ship time."

Four hours.

"Luse," the Sarerl said, instantly losing any hints of playfulness. "Yogodvos Marta. Prepare to switch to Yogodvos Kasna at ship time 20:30. Senior Gunnery Officer, perform tactical analysis. I want to know our odds in advance."

Normally, Lexshu wouldn't have asked, but the extra crew members, Jarluk Dreu, and Lartnei were on her mind.

In his room, Jinto battled a formidable adversary: the book of Administrative Students' Lifestyle Regulations (Lyuel Kunasot Kenrur Sazoir). Among the Lodair of the Recruitment Office, the commonly held belief was that all students were expected to memorize the rules before enrolling.

It's no use . . . Jinto really had no idea what he was getting himself into when the man at the Recruitment Office had handed him the computer crystal.

He said the dirtiest Delktou word he knew.

Whoever wrote these regulations opted not to eliminate the outdated ones, but to amend them with confusing addendums. The footnotes were more numerous than the regulations; it wasn't uncommon to read through a page only to find that such-and-such regulation was abolished some time ago.

I'll never learn this by next month.

He was totally screwed! He had to learn it — it was his duty — but before he boarded the *Gosroth*, he'd never even glanced at it.

Wondering how many rules he'd broken in his first few days aboard the ship, Jinto began to read the section on dining hall manners. Thinking ahead, he peeked at the end and checked if the regulations were still in effect. Satisfied, he continued to read, skimming the obvious, regretting his blunders from the previous days' meals.

Just when Jinto hit his studying groove, the alarm bell rang. He looked up from his Kreuno's projection screen.

What the hell was that?

Before he could even look it up in the Lyuel's index, shipwide announcements began.

"Attention. Sarerl here. There is an unknown group of Flasath cruising seventy-eight degrees ahead of our ship, approximately fifteen hundred forty Kedlairl away. Their destination appears to be the same as ours, the Loebehynu Sufagnaum."

After allowing an appropriate amount of time for this news to sink in, the Sarerl continued, "Now, we are definitely in a position to reach Safugnoff first. They don't seem to like that idea, as they've sent ten Flasath ships our way. We are not sure where they came from, but evidence points to the United Mankind. This means war."

Is this a drill? Jinto asked himself.

"This is not a drill," Lexshu answered the unspoken question. "I repeat — this is not a drill. If they do not yield, battle will begin at approximately 21:25 ship time. Thus, we're scheduled to switch to Yogodvos Kasna at 20:30 ship time. Now, my friends, at the risk of being annoyingly repetitive, this is not a drill. Sarerl out."

Staring at the ceiling, Jinto tried to digest the announcement.

We're going into battle. It all seemed very sudden.

As far as Jinto knew, the Frybar wasn't even engaged in any disputes anywhere. Furthermore, they were in Abh territory. This should have been nothing but smooth sailing.

Jinto stared at the banner, but it offered no answers.

He looked back at the projection screen. Although he wasn't sure what to do, somehow studying didn't seem appropriate. Jinto cleared the Kreuno.

He hesitated to run to the bridge, or to call someone and get more info. Even if he knew what was going on, he doubted he could be of any use.

"Jinto, are you there?" Lafiel's voice came through the intercom.

Leaping up, Jinto answered her call. "Of course I'm here. Come in, Lafiel!"

The door opened, but Lafiel remained in the entrance.

"What does it all mean?" he asked quietly.

"Just what they said. I don't know anything more than that," Lafiel said. "I think we're in the wrong place at the wrong time. Apparently, this is where a war is starting."

"Lucky us," Jinto mumbled. "I hope it ends soon."

"Fat chance," Lafiel said. "We don't do war half-assed. And this time, the opponent appears to be the United Mankind . . . Well, I doubt this will end before I die."

Jinto grimaced. "You're a real ray of sunshine, you know that?"

"I've been ordered to bring you to the Gahorl. Can you come right away?"

"Yes, yes, of course." As he stood up, Jinto put the crown of Jarluk Dreu Haider on his head. "Think they'll have a seat for me?"

"Why don't you ask them?"

When they arrived on the bridge, the tension was palpable.

"I'm very sorry to make you come up here, Lonyu," Lexshu greeted him. "Bene Lodair Abriel, you wait there, too."

"Yes, ma'am." Lafiel stood at attention behind Jinto.

"Unfortunately, Lonyu Jarluk Dreu, I don't have a seat ready for you," the Hecto-Commander said from the captain's chair.

He smiled. "Don't sweat it. I'm fine with standing."

"I assume you're up to speed after the onboard announcement."

"Yes. We're headed for war."

Nodding, the Sarerl said, "Our probability of winning is a mere point thirty-seven percent. That figure assumes we're up against a topnotch enemy. But even if they were raw recruits in decrepit ships, our chances of winning wouldn't be more than five percent."

"Rough," Jinto said calmly, despite the fact that he was facing imminent death.

"Yes. Escape would be optimal, but is simply not possible." The Sarerl smiled. "But I do insist that Lonyu Jarluk Haider get off the ship."

"I see." Jinto nodded. Though less than heroic, her proposal made sense.

The operation of Menyu, or spaceships, required a glut of high-level skills. The crew, even the lowest class (Sash Gorna), all had more than a year of special training. Even if Jinto, who had no training whatsoever, were assigned a noble duty, all he could do was tremble in fear and get in the way.

There was only one problem—they were in Plane Space. *How can I get off the patrol ship, and where will I go?* Jinto wondered.

"There is a contact vessel onboard the ship. It's a small Pelia, but it is equipped with Menraj, which means you can use it to travel through Plane Space to Safugnoff. You won't be able to get any supplies once you're on your way, but you should make it to Safugnoff before the Flasath group. Once there, you'll need to find a new ship. There are many fleet communication bases on Safugnoff." Lexshu glanced behind Jinto. "Bene Lodair Abriel will take you to Loebehynu Sufagnaum."

"But Sarerl!" Lafiel protested. "I don't have a pilot's badge."

"You've finished your pilot's coursework," the Hecto-Commander pointed out. "After this cruise is over, you can get your Busespas automatically. It's all standard procedure from here on out. You can steer, Bene."

"But I'm on *this* ship—"

"I don't intend to argue with a pilot trainee. I am the Sarerl of this ship," Lexshu said smartly.

"I can't do it." Lafiel wouldn't budge. "It would bring shame upon the Abriel name if I ran away."

The captain stood up, glaring at Lafiel with her sharp, golden eyes. "Save the speeches until you've got a two-winged tiara, Abriel Nei Debrusc Viscountess Lafiel. You're not running away, because this is not *your* battle. You are surplus crew on this ship. And I'm giving you a duty, an important one. You will remove Lonyu Jarluk Dreu, a noncombatant, from danger and inform the Frybar of these events. To shirk this responsibility would bring an equal amount of shame on the Abriel family. If you say anything further, I'll hold you for disobeying orders, at which point the Luzei Fanigalak will charge you formally."

Biting her lip hard, Lafiel paled. Yet her eyes continued to battle the Sarerl's gaze. The whole exchange made Jinto undeniably anxious.

The Lartnei folded. "I misunderstood, Sarerl."

"If you understand, then fine." Lexshu nodded. "Prepare to launch the Pelia immediately. I need to speak with Lonyu Jarluk Dreu."

"Roger." Lafiel saluted. "I will prepare the Pelia for launch."

The captain relaxed slightly. "Report back when it's ready, but you needn't come back here."

"Understood."

They continued to stare at each other for a moment.

"Good. Now, go," Lexshu said kindly. "We'll meet again on Lakfakalle, My Lovely Highness."

"Without question." Although it seemed like she had more to say, Lafiel spun on her heel and left.

Once Lafiel was gone, the Hecto-Commander turned to Jinto. "Lonyu Jarluk Dreu, time and space are limited. Please take only necessary personal goods."

Jinto nodded. "I can get the rest at the Arosh."

"I'm very sorry I couldn't deliver you on schedule."

He shrugged. "Sometimes there's traffic. What can you do?"

"It's a relief to hear you say that. One more thing, Lonyu Jarluk Dreu."

"What's that?"

"I want you to take something with you." Lexshu turned to the wall behind the captain's seat. "Open small arms safe. Bomowas Lexshu Wef-Robell Plakia."

The wall opened, revealing an impressive array of hand-held weapons.

It was a breach of etiquette for a Labule Lodair to carry a weapon while on a ship. Thus, they kept their personal arsenal in Kutaroev.

However, the captain had to be prepared for anything, including a mutiny—which hadn't happened in the Frybar for over two hundred years. Even so, captains always kept a few weapons on board.

Lexshu selected two laser pistols (Klanyu), and presented them with holsters and ammo (Japer). "One is for Lonyu. Please give the other to Bene Lodair Abriel. She will know how to use them."

"Think we'll need them?" Jinto asked as he accepted the guns.

"It's just a precaution." The Sarerl glanced at the Ja Flasath on the floor screen. "That's probably the front line of an enemy invasion fleet. If it weren't, there'd be no reason to divide their forces to stop us. They're definitely looking for trouble."

Jinto inhaled sharply. "Based on the odds, by the time we reach Safugnoff, you'll probably be destroyed."

"I pray it isn't so, but . . ." The Hecto-Commander smiled.

"Sarerl," Jinto began, finally realizing Lexshu's true intention. "You really wanted to let Feia Lartneir escape, right? Even though she's probably much more suited to guard duty than I am."

Once the golden eyes gazed on him, Jinto stopped talking.

"Don't misinterpret. It is necessary to evacuate as many non-combat personnel as possible. It is a fact that Bene Lodair Abriel has no fixed *battle* duty post. Even if she were a nameless Lef, I would have issued the same orders."

"Sorry, I've said something stupid."

"Just between us," Lexshu whispered, "I'd be a liar if I said I wasn't pleased by the coincidence."

He hesitated. "You care about her, don't you, Sarerl?"

"Yes. Even though I said social status doesn't matter when you're in the military, Feia Lafiel is a person who

may become Spunej. She could even be a great Empress.
And at that time, I hope she will recognize the outstanding
education she received as a Bene . . . I should let you go.
Please pack your things. I'm sorry I can't guide you. You
know the way to the Goriaav, don't you?"

"I'll be okay," Jinto responded. "Hey, you know my
family's banner that you guys prepared for me? I'll leave it
here for now, but I look forward to the day when I can get
it back as a memento of being on board."

"That's very noble of you, Lonyu."

"Really? Awesome." Jinto bowed. "Please excuse me,
Sarerl."

Lexshu paused. "Look after Feia Lartneir."

"I can't really imagine any straits dire enough that
Feia would have to rely on *me*, but if we come to any, I'll
do my best."

"The Pelia has departed."

Bomowas Lexshu nodded her approval of the communications officer's announcement.

Essential personnel tensely filed into the Gahorl. The Labule prided itself on maintaining at least the façade of fearlessness. No one aboard the *Gosroth* had any real battle experience, so they were understandably anxious.

Luse Reilia was the first to regain his calm. "The boy and girl are gone," he said to the Sarerl from his seat positioned diagonally behind the captain's chair.

"I hope they make it." Lexshu rested her chin in her hands as she watched the little blue light grow fainter.

"Yes." Reilia chuckled. "They're pretty funny now. I can only imagine how hilarious they'll be in the future."

They were quite an odd pair, the stereotypical Abh and the lander nobleman.

"Maybe they'll have a good influence on each other," Reilia added.

"You know, Reilia," Lexshu turned to her Luse, "you sound like a teacher. Are you trying to transfer to the Kenru?"

"Don't be absurd," he said, waving his hand. "I'm definitely not equipped to be a Besega—I'll take a battle any day. I'm much more at home on the front lines."

Lexshu grinned. "Coward."

"That's what I'd consider someone who asks for a transfer to the rear. But I have no intention of doing that, Sarerl."

"That's a shame," the captain said.

"Am I that bad a Luse?" Reilia joked.

Beaming, Lexshu shot back, "Let's just say I'd rather see you in front of a classroom." A pause. "Professor Reilia, what did you think of Lonyu Jarluk Dreu?"

"Seems like a good guy to me. In all my interactions with him, he kept looking at me like he wanted me to verify that he was doing everything to Abh standards. I'll never forget that look."

Suddenly, Lexshu snorted. "He flung so many questions my way—I'm telling you, I've never thought about our character as much as I did in these last five days."

"As a Lef, he should learn to be more restrained."

"He means well, though."

Reilia nodded. "True. I think knowing the Lonyu will be good for Feia."

"Yes. Bringing them together may go down as my greatest achievement. Assuming they make it to the capital alive."

"You're really worried about them, huh?" Reilia prodded.

"Is that weird?" Lexshu was not amused.

"Well, although it pains me to criticize a superior officer, I don't think this is the right time to worry about *them*. We're the ones in trouble. That's why we sent them away, remember?"

"For someone who doesn't like to criticize, you sure talk a lot." The Sarerl glanced at the little blips of light on her monitor. "But you make a good point. Duty first."

19:37 Ship Time

"Oh no," the forward communications officer declared. "This is not a communication! It's Aga Izomia—a challenge to battle!"

A few moments earlier, the Flasath group had entered communications range. The Sarerl had Communications Officer Lekle Yunseryuna issue a Drosh Flacteder that identified the *Gosroth* and requested the Flasath group's name and directive.

After a few tense moments, the answer came back: *Aga Izomia.*

Expelling the last bit of hope that the Flasath group was an allied fleet with secret orders, Lexshu sighed. "Affirmative." Oddly, she felt slightly relieved.

"They're sending battle challenge continuously. Should we reply?"

"Forget it. What they don't know can't hurt us."

On all display screens, the Flasath group changed colors from blue to a more hostile-looking red. The red blips crept continually closer.

20:30 Ship Time

Clang! Clang!

A Duniit echoed throughout the ship.

"Attention. This is your Sarerl. The unknown Flasath are confirmed to be hostile. Switch to Yogodvos Kasna immediately. All hands put on your Saput and prepare for battle!"

Completely ignoring the captain's order, no one on the bridge bothered to put on a space helmet. Because the Flasath creation engine (Flasatia) was directly under the bridge, the same spherical wall encased it. If the airtight seal in the bridge were breached, the ship would already be toast. Thus it was an unwritten rule that those on the bridge didn't need to wear bulky Saput.

"Battle preparations complete. All hands ready," Luse Reilia announced.

"Prepare for Hoksatjocs," said the Sarerl. "Fill Hoksath numbers seven through ten with antimatter fuel."

Sates Gor Hoksat, commonly called Hoksath, were mines equipped with miniature engines. So, despite the fact that they were unmanned, they were technically considered small Menyu. The *Gosroth* could only carry ten at a time and had already used six in training exercises.

Antimatter annihilation propelled the Hoksath and also gave them their explosive power. It was dangerous to keep them loaded with antimatter fuel (called Baish), so they had to fill them up from the ship's antimatter fuel tank before every use.

Supervisor Lowas Skem Gumrua oversaw fuel transfers. At his command, the antiprotons filtered through magnetic tubes into the mine deck, where they flowed into the four Hoksath magnetic containers.

"Antimatter fuel replenishment complete," Senior Gunnery Officer Lekle Saryush relayed from the mine deck.

"Launch Hoksath. Generate Flasath and stand by."

The ship released the four mines into space, where they slowly began to rotate in their own little menacing space-time bubbles.

21:30 Ship Time

Closing in with alarming speed, the enemy Flasath spread out to surround the *Gosroth*.

"Classic attack formation," Lexshu said, unimpressed.

By this time, the enemy Flasath group had entered the limited range of the display on the Sarerl's Latonyu. Ideally, Lexshu would like to have had two mines for every ship. This day, she would have to improvise.

Looking at the screen, she quickly decided how to proceed. "Hoksath alignment: seven to three; eight to one; nine to six; ten to seven."

"Factors inputted." For some reason, the Tlakia Hoksak made everyone nervous whenever he spoke, perhaps because he was so tense. "Alignment complete."

Switching her tiara to external input, Lexshu's Frokaj took over and she lost all sense of being on the bridge. Once the information from the ship's sensors flowed into her Rilbido, it was as though she were floating in the center of a sphere, watching the Flasath. The inner surface of Flasath glowed an ashy gray from collisions with Supflasath. It was eerily calm.

"Prepare for Dadjocs. Battle in normal space will be just as hard! Ignite Opsei."

"Roger. Igniting Opsei," Gumrua repeated.

As antimatter and matter collided in the main engines, the *Gosroth* shook noticeably.

Hopefully none of the crew consider it an omen, the captain thought. "Prepare the Irgyuf, Gunnery Officer!"

"Roger. Preparing Irgyuf to fire." Lekle Saryush, whose job was to navigate within the Flasath, put on a Gooheik. With his empty right hand, the flight officer released the electromagnetic projection cannon's safety switch. With another push of a button, he loaded the weapon. "The electromagnetic projection cannon is ready to fire."

On Lexshu's monitor, the enemy continued to encircle the *Gosroth*, a swarm of red dots ganging up on their lonely blue dot.

Classic. Lexshu admired the opponent. She knew it was extremely difficult to hold such a tight formation inside Plane Space, which hindered communication. *They are obviously well trained. But if training alone determines the victor, they don't have a chance.*

Although the *Gosroth* had only entered service three months earlier, giving the crew scant time to train, they were all highly skilled officers.

21:32 Ship Time

"My lovelies," Lexshu addressed all hands via the Luode on the Latonyu. "Let's get this party started."

Pulling her Greu from her belt like a samurai drawing a sword, Lexshu stood. The captain's seat retracted into the floor. "Saparga!"

Alarms sounded.

Lexshu bravely thrust out her chin. Using her Greu, she pointed to the Tlakia Hoksak. "Detach all Hoksath."

"Detaching Hoksath," echoed the gunnery officer. "Number seven, Gor Lyutcoth. Eight, Gor Lyutcoth. Nine . . ."

One by one, the Hoksath flew out of Frokaj range. Lexshu had to use her Latonyu, which looked like a preschooler's rendering of battle—four blue dots flew toward four red dots.

"Number eight, Gor Putarloth. Enemy Flasath number one annihilated!"

Everyone cheered.

(It would have been impossible for anyone aboard the *Gosroth* to know it, but the enemy ship wrapped in Flasath was one of the United Mankind's destroyer spaceships, *KE03799*. Its captain, Lieutenant Kartsen, and its twenty-three crew members eventually went into the record books as the first casualties of the long war that followed.)

Hoksath numbers seven and ten each downed an enemy. As the enemy Flasath blew apart, they struck the Supflasath, causing a ripple in Plane Space.

Hoksath number nine, unfortunately, underperformed. The enemy's number six Flasath continued to close in as though it didn't have a care in the world.

"Change heading forty degrees starboard!" Lexshu gesticulated wildly with the Greu, directing Rilbiga Flaktlaushsasiar, who was in charge of Flasath motion control.

By that time, the enemy implemented Gor Putarloth from multiple directions, intending to gang up on the patrol ship. It was a solid strategy, proven effective in many battles. The *Gosroth*, however, did not intend to go down without a fight.

"Ram enemy number four!"

"Roger," the Rilbiga replied.

The *Gosroth* flew toward number four.

"Distance—less than one hundred Sheskedlerl. Fifty Sheskedlerl . . ."

"Fuse space-time upon impact."

By that time, the Sarerl's Frokaj could already detect the collision between the inner surface and a large amount of Supflasath.

"Aim the ship's bow at the fusion surface." Lexshu thrust her Greu at the ominously rumbling surface. "As soon as we fuse, fire without waiting for my order."

"Got it," Saryush said.

"All hands prepare for Irgyuf volley," the Luse warned the entire crew.

The ship's prow bashed into the bubbling surface.

"Gor Putarloth!"

As the ship collided with the Flasath, a huge tunnel opened, revealing a separate tiny universe containing the enemy spaceship.

As soon as they recognized the tunnel, Saryush didn't need to be told what to do. The *Gosroth* had six Irgyuf—four forward and two aft. Upon entering the tunnel, Saryush fired the front four simultaneously.

Spewing nuclear fusion shells (Spyut) at a hundredth of the speed of light, the cannons caused the whole ship to recoil violently. Despite Lexshu's warning, crew members who weren't strapped in fell over.

Lexshu clutched the Latonyu to keep from falling.

In an entirely defensive maneuver, the enemy peppered the air with decoy spray, trying to ward off the Spyut. When that failed, the enemy attempted to counterattack with its own antiproton cannon.

Luckily, the magnetic field encasing the *Gosroth* easily deflected the antiproton stream, redirecting it into the vacuum of space.

KA-BOOM.

The enemy ship was terminated.

There was no time to celebrate, however; the inner surface of the Flasath was already showing preliminary indications of Gor Putarloth in six places. It was like an old horror film—as soon as the *Gosroth* successfully locked the front door, the zombies began climbing through the back windows.

"We've got space-time fusion with enemies number two, five, six . . ."

"Bow, here!" Lexshu pointed at the fusion with enemy Flasath number two, which she suspected would complete fusion the fastest.

The ship's nose turned quickly. Right before the tunnel opened, the *Gosroth* fired. Without waiting for the results, they switched focus to the next target, the enemy Flasath almost directly behind them.

"Stern, here!" Lexshu pointed over her shoulder with the Greu. The *Gosroth* shifted position. Cannons fired.

Aware of the *Gosroth's* electromagnetic blast, the sixth enemy ship detached as soon as fusion was complete. Their escape effort was futile, however, because two of the shots entered the tunnel during its split-second opening, and right after number six detached, it exploded.

Then enemy Flasath five achieved fusion from the flank and there was no way the *Gosroth* could turn fast enough to shoot it.

Lexshu sliced the air with her Greu. "Support with mobile gun battery."

Upon her command, gunners on the bridge manually aimed the ship's smaller laser cannons (Voklanyu) and antiproton cannons (Lenyj). Without further instruction, the gunners barraged the enemy with Klanraj and antiprotons.

However, neither the lasers nor the antiproton streams were equipped with automatic guidance systems, so their hit-to-miss ratios were understandably lower than that of the electromagnetic shell cannons. On top of that, they were not as powerful.

The enemy ship deployed four antimatter missiles and then fired its Lenyj.

The *Gosroth* easily dispatched the enemy's ballistic missiles with defensive counter-fire. However, the enemy ship also let loose a monstrous antiproton blast, which greatly overpowered the *Gosroth's* secondary artillery.

The *Gosroth's* Sneseb field slowed the antiproton stream enough that the blast didn't completely destroy the ship. However, it did knock the *Gosroth* for a loop and pierce the ship's Ryabon outer hull, causing all the water in the inner barrier's walls to boil. The boiling water erupted from the ship's attitude-control jets.

One of the attitude-control jets was now worthless, drastically decreasing the ship's maneuverability!

23:05 Ship Time

Enemy ship number ten was annihilated! Only two enemy ships left.

Unfortunately, the *Gosroth* suffered major damage; almost half of its mobile gun batteries were silent and several of its attitude-control jets were damaged.

"Voklanyu number two destroyed!"

"Forward jet three unusable!"

"Opsei's output . . ."

Damage reports poured in continuously from every direction.

Gumrua assembled emergency repair teams and prioritized their operations. Some parts of the ship were beyond repair.

"Section nine depressurizing! There's no one there. I'm sealing it off." Diesh wiped beads of sweat from his brow.

With over forty sections sealed off, and fifty of the ship's two hundred and twenty Sash unaccounted for, the *Gosroth* was in sorry shape.

Lexshu closed her eyes, cleared her Frosh.

Debris—fragments of decimated ships—littered the space around the *Gosroth*. Although there might have been survivors among the wreckage, the *Gosroth* couldn't risk sending anyone out to retrieve them. A Serlin simply wasn't thick enough to protect the body from the radioactive crossfire going on out there.

Frustratingly agile, the two enemy ships circled the *Gosroth* like angry wasps, ceaselessly spitting stingers.

Lexshu tried to catch them with the Irgyuf, but the *Gosroth* was too slow for this to work. The gunners never let up with the Klanraj.

Direct hit! A piece blew off one enemy ship's outer hull.

Ionized hydrogen from the enemy's propulsion jets increased the particle density inside its Flasath. Floating protons and antiprotons collided, turning into electromagnetic waves. The small, closed universe heated to temperatures comparable to the big bang—Driaron.

However, this heat didn't mark the birth of a universe, but the death of one—an entire Flasath was obliterated.

Fragments of the ship exploded into the firing range of the rear Irgyuf.

"Stern!" Lexshu commanded.

The cannons fired, reducing the last remnants of the enemy ship to a burning sphere.

One ship left.

The final enemy fired Lenyj from one side. It was a good shot.

Gumrua gasped. "Sneseb destroyed."

Despair blanketed the bridge.

"Don't give up, my lovelies!" Lexshu reprimanded. "We'll blow that thing out of the universe. The bow!"

The *Gosroth* laboriously changed direction, creaking and groaning.

"Mobile gun batteries, fire at will on the enemy's starboard side."

The enemy spaceship continued to advance on the *Gosroth*, firing Lenyj the whole time.

An unprecedented flood of antiprotons barreled toward the almost defenseless *Gosroth*.

The mobile guns cut down the enemy's hull, but that barely slowed it down.

The next antiproton blast pierced the inner hull of the *Gosroth* and knocked over the antimatter fuel tank (or Baikok). The tank's magnetic cage burst, and the antiprotons began to eat away at the patrol ship . . .

At 23:27 ship time, the *Gosroth* exploded.

Lafiel and Jinto didn't know of the *Gosroth's* defeat. Even if Sesuwas communications could travel that far, the Pelia's crude instruments wouldn't be able to receive the mass waves. On top of that, there was a Sord in the way.

All things considered, their ignorance was probably for the best. The Pelia's Shirsh Sediar was gloomy enough without adding to it a sense of tremendous loss. At least this way they still had hope.

Jinto squirmed uncomfortably in the copilot's seat.

Unlike a Kalique, a Pelia required more than just a Gooheik to navigate through Fath. There were steering instruments, devices, and switches.

In the pilot's seat, Lafiel remained silent and focused.

Jinto stole a glance in her direction and sighed.

Aside from a smattering of random particles, the Pelia was the only thing inside the little bubble of the Flasath. There was an airlock (Yadobel) behind the Pelia's steering room and behind that, a lavatory and nap room. And those were the only options for human habitation in the universe.

"Um, Lafiel?" Jinto hoped to start a conversation.

Lafiel raised her head ambiguously.

Bravely, Jinto pushed ahead. "You're a viscountess, right?"

"Yes."

"What's your Ribeun like? I mean, what kind of place is Parhynu? That means Country of Roses, right? Are there a ton of roses, or what?"

"No, it's a misnomer." Although she seemed less than interested in the topic, Lafiel humored him. "There aren't roses. There aren't lichens. There aren't even any microbes on any of the planets."

"So why is it called Parhynu?"

"The man who discovered it liked flowers. He gave everything a flower name; Gryhynu, Speshynu, and so forth."

He shook his head. "What a crock. So what's it like?"

"There's nothing special about it. There's one yellow star with seven orbiting planets. With a lot of sprucing up, the second planet could potentially be inhabitable. I might take that on as a project once I'm released from my Fasanzoerl obligations. I'd like to make that planet resemble its name."

"Sounds like a great plan."

"I guess."

Again, silence settled over the small, enclosed space.

Jinto wracked his brains for a way to end the unbearable quiet, but he was drawing a blank.

Luckily, Lafiel bailed him out. "Jinto."

"Yes?"

"Thank you."

"What? Why?"

"For caring about me. Although you're not the most refined person I've ever met," she batted her long eyelashes,

"I appreciate your interest and enthusiasm."

"I'm not entirely sure how to take that."

"It's a good thing." Lafiel smiled. "Don't be mad."

"Okay."

Lafiel stared at the screen sullenly. "I wish there was something I could have done back there."

"You *are* doing something—you're saving my butt. Doesn't that mean anything?"

She paused. "Forgive me. You're right."

"I'm sure the ship will be okay. I know it," Jinto said—although he had no real reason to think so.

"Yeah."

"Yeah," Jinto repeated, mostly to convince himself.

"Jinto, remember my birth secret?"

"Of course." *Am I crazy, or did that come completely out of the blue?*

"Can you keep a secret? Just between us?"

"I love secrets!" Jinto was doing his best to brighten things up, hoping to improve the Lartnei's mood.

"My Larliin was the Sarerl."

"What?" Jinto poked a finger into his ear to make sure it hadn't malfunctioned. "So Hecto-Commander Lexshu was your mother?"

"Not my mother. My Larliin."

"Sorry. You can take a lander out of a solar system . . ." He didn't bother to finish the old expression. "Wow. I never would have guessed."

On second thought, I should have known. He remembered their departure, when the captain had called Lafiel "My Lovely Highness." It gave a new weight to their dispute.

"Oh dear. This is all very complex." Jinto threw his hands up.

"I was privileged to know Kyua Plakia from the time I was a child. And I'm proud to think that half of me comes from her. Maybe I was a Fryum Neg after all—maybe she was my father's ideal mate."

"If you've known her so long, why didn't you try asking her?" Jinto scratched his head. The Abh's distinction between family and genetic relations confused him.

Lafiel just stared at Jinto.

"What, do I have boogers or something? Did I say something weird? What's wrong with asking the Sarerl directly?"

"The Abh have something, I don't know if you've heard of it—it's called 'manners.' "

"Ha! You're telling me it's rude to ask your Larliin whether she's your Larliin?"

"Yes. Extremely."

"Really?" Jinto asked. He didn't get it at all. "Why is that rude?"

"Why is it rude to interrupt someone? It just is."

I guess it's not so weird. I probably wouldn't go up to someone and ask, "Are you my mother?"

"Even if I asked, she wouldn't tell me. Only a parent can tell his child about her Delrash."

"That's etiquette, huh?"

"Yes."

He shook his head again. "So complicated."

"I don't think so."

"I want to take you to my old home once, and see you adjust to the customs there. Then you'll see why I think it's complicated."

"How about after I finish my Fasanzoerl duties?" Lafiel asked playfully.

"You got it," Jinto agreed, thinking about the future.

By that time, even if you haven't forgotten this conversation, you'll barely have aged. And I'll be old and decrepit, or maybe even dead.

"But, you said the Sarerl was your father's . . ." he searched for the word, ". . . Larth Kryb Feia's Yofu—His Majesty's ideal person? If you asked that, it'd be okay to tell you, right?"

"Of course not."

Jinto frowned. "Even though you think she was?"

"Exactly. Is that complicated, too?"

"Extremely! Who told you that Bomowas Lexshu was Larth Kryb Feia's lover?"

"I just knew. The Sarerl often came to the Lartbei."

"Wow. This is all blowing my mind."

"Can we change the subject please?" Lafiel frowned.

"Sorry." He shrugged.

Opening her mouth as if to speak, Lafiel turned to Jinto. After a second, she turned back to the screen. Only then did she say, "Even if I weren't her descendent, I love Kyua Plakia. I respected her in the Lartbei, and even more aboard the ship. And the other Lodair and Sash all did too. I truly hope they're all okay." As if praying, Lafiel hung her head.

"Yeah." Jinto reflected on his five short days aboard the ship. In that small amount of time, he hadn't met a single person he didn't like. In his limited experience, all the rumors and stereotypes claiming the Abh were Imperial tyrants so far proven completely unfounded.

The heavy atmosphere that Jinto had wanted to assuage settled on them again.

At last, Lafiel looked up. "Jinto," she implored, "tell me about your homeworld."

"Oh, you bet." Jinto blew a huge sigh of relief. "Where to begin? Unlike the desolate hunk of rock you call a Ribeun, there's actually a lot to describe."

Searching for inspiration, Jinto noticed that he was nervously fiddling with the fake jewel on his chest. He decided to talk about the creature carved on it—the Lezwan—and its unusual eating habits.

Over the course of the next two days, except when they took turns napping, Jinto chattered on about Planet Martine and all the creatures living there. Occasionally, he inserted a memory or made an exaggeration. He even managed to get Lafiel to laugh a few times.

Then, after two days inside the Pelia, Jinto and Lafiel arrived in Lyumusko Febdak.

Lyumusko Febdak sucked.

Comprised of one blue star, two gaseous planets, and countless bits of rocky debris, it was not exactly fit to be the tourism capital of the universe. Even with the most advanced terraforming technology the Frybar had, it was impossible to make a habitable planet there, and there weren't enough resources in the asteroids to bother transporting them.

In short, this star system had even more *nothing* than Parhynu.

However, the Lyumjhe had found a way to do business there—if there was a fixed star, the family found that there was money to be made.

Even in this star system with no resources, there were numerous profitable antimatter fuel factories (Joth).

Antimatter manufacture was an ancient process. The first step in converting matter to antimatter was to collect a fixed star's radiation with solar batteries, then to pour that energy into a linear accelerator. Accelerated elementary particles struck each other at speeds great enough to create small quantities of antimatter.

Once manufactured, the antiprotons went into containers connected to the Joth. When a container was full, it was placed further into orbit as an independent asteroid to prevent cataclysmic meltdowns.

Like a flock of frisbee moons, the disc-shaped Joth orbited the star of Febdash. Even farther in orbit than the fuel tank asteriods, the Sord was right next to the Lyumex Febdak.

A single Pelia entered normal space through the Sord.

"Can you please show the view outside, Lafiel?" Jinto asked.

"Sure." Her Gooheik-clad hand contorted into an unnatural shape, and the wall of the Shirsh Sediar became a blanket of stars.

"Wow. I never thought I'd be so happy to see stars," Jinto said wholeheartedly. For two days, he'd seen nothing but the gloomy gray interior of the Flasath. He suddenly understood why the Abh called themselves Kasarl Gereulak and considered space their home.

"We still have a long way to go, Jinto," Lafiel said woodenly. "We'll have to return to Plane Space immediately after resupplying."

"Do we get to take a break while we resupply?" Jinto asked hopefully.

"You say that like you've been working really hard."

Jinto pretended to be hurt. "Hey, who kept an eye on all this equipment while you slept?"

"You woke me up whenever anything happened."

"I did not. Nothing ever happened."

"Thanks to me and my Datykirl."

"I can't dispute that." He really couldn't.

It was entirely true that Jinto hadn't done anything. The Pelia had a sophisticated autopilot. He never even saw Lafiel steer.

He sighed. "I did carry the conversation. That's got to count for something."

Rolling her eyes, Lafiel hailed the controller. "This is the Resii *Gosroth's* Pelia. Space Traffic Control Lyumusko Febdak, please respond."

A lander woman appeared on the monitor.

"This is Control Lyumusko Febdak."

"Hello. We are the Resii *Gosroth's* Pelia. Requesting refueling."

"A Resii's Pelia, you say?" The controller seemed surprised to find a warship's small craft refueling by itself. Regardless, she nodded. "Roger, *Gosroth's* Pelia. Welcome. Please select your form of supply."

"This is a Menyu Sorna. We request supply at one of the docks."

"Roger. Will you please transmit the amount of fuel you want?"

"Roger." As soon as Lafiel finished transmitting some data, she turned to Jinto. "If it's a dock supply, we can rest. Maybe even bathe."

"Oh, great!" Jinto's eyes lit up. "A hot bath is probably a good idea. Right now, you're probably the smelliest Lartnei in the galaxy."

"Excuse me?" Lafiel's eyes narrowed. "Did you just say that you'd like to die? I can help you with that."

"Sheesh. I'm just kidding." Jinto smiled mischievously. "I mean, you're not *that* smelly."

Lafiel's eyes narrowed further.

"Okay, okay. You don't smell at all." She didn't really, and he hadn't meant to make her angry.

Lafiel pulled her shirt to her nose, inhaled, then grimaced. "Okay, you're not too far out of line."

Discretely, Jinto smiled.

"Although, I probably just soaked up some of your residual stench."

"Ha!" Jinto acknowledged, but before he could say anything else, the controller reappeared on the screen.

"Everything's in order. We've granted you dock supply, *Gosroth's* Pelia. Proceed to the pier at once . . ." the controller trailed off and squinted suspiciously. Suddenly, her eyes popped open. "Feia Lartneir?"

The controller bowed, shocked to discover the Sedia's identity.

Wow, Jinto thought, *they even recognize her in a remote region like this. I must have seemed like an even bigger hick than I thought.*

"Can you guide me to the Bes?" Lafiel asked.

"The dock? Of course I can. At once. Yes."

With the aid of the tense controller's data, the Pelia connected to the Lyumex.

"Belyse Lyumusko Febdak, I have a report for you." While they docked at the Lyumex, Lafiel relayed the intrusion of the enemy fleet into Frybar territory.

"But that's . . ." The controller couldn't continue. After a moment, she recovered. "I'll inform my master."

"Please do."

That's when Jinto caught his first glimpse of the Lyumex, a cube-shaped building suspended in the middle of an enormous hexagonal frame. There were a few small, interstellar transport ships docked at the spaceport like insects on a log. Most of the orbital mansions (Garish) were ring-shaped because they relied on rotational pseudo-gravity — newer Garish employed Wameria to combat the variations in gravitational pull.

Shortly after the Pelia docked, the mansion's artificial gravity kicked in and the spherical steering room began to rotate.

They approached the seventeenth Bes and docked. The outside view disappeared, and the walls returned to their original milky white. Green letters streamed across the screen, announcing the junction tube's connection to the Lo.

"Let's go, Jinto." Lafiel took off her navigation equipment and stood up.

Jinto also stood. "How long will we be here?"

"Maybe thirty minutes."

"That's it?" Jinto frowned. He wished for more time to clean up. *Oh well. Thirty minutes beats a kick in the pants.*

"We have to reach Safugnoff as soon as possible."

"Right." Jinto followed Lafiel into the Yadobel. "How much earlier than the enemy fleet will we arrive?"

"About twenty-seven hours, by Safugnoff time," Lafiel said, as if the answer were more obvious than breathing.

"That's not much time at all."

On the Lo Yadobel, they stepped onto a waiting Feretocork.

"Descend," Lafiel commanded.

Once lowered through the junction tube, they stepped into the Lyumex. Gravity—after two days without it—made Jinto dizzy.

Inside the Lyumex, the view was undoubtedly manufactured—in addition to the star of Febdash remaining visible from every angle, countless fish swam among the stars.

Dozens of landers stood in rows in front of the junction tube—probably the Lyuf's vassals.

Vassals are called Gosuk, Jinto reminded himself. Something about the whole scene bothered Jinto. At first, he couldn't put his finger on it. Then he realized. *They're all female!*

The women bowed their heads.

"Feia Lartneir." The controller walked forward respectfully. As if she were afraid that looking directly at the Spunej's granddaughter would scorch her eyes, she kept her gaze on the floor. "Please come this way. I'll guide you to the lounge."

"I have a favor to ask you." Lafiel's tone was strong. "I am now a pilot trainee in the Labule, and I'd like you to regard me as such, with no more or less respect."

"Yes, of course. This way, please, Feia Lartneir."

Lafiel sighed.

The guide led them into a room inside the spaceport facility. There were tables and the same eerie space-fish murals. No one else was in the room.

The controller placed Lafiel at the innermost seat. Jinto went to sit next to her, but the controller stopped him. "Please take this seat instead!"

"Okay," Jinto said, looking around the otherwise empty room. "I didn't realize that one was taken."

"That's . . ." The controller mumbled something, diffidently avoiding Jinto's eyes.

He'd have to get used to that reaction—the combination of brown hair and an Imperial noble's crown were sure to draw that response all over the universe. Surely a lander shouldn't sit next to a member of the Spunej's family.

"Jinto!" Lafiel snapped him out of his reverie. "Sit down already."

"Yes, ma'am." Jinto deliberately ignored the controller and sat down.

The controller frowned momentarily, then asked Lafiel if she wanted something to drink.

"More than a drink," said Lafiel, "I'd like to use a Shirsh Guzar. Is there one available?"

"Fasanzoerl, use a shower?" The controller's eyes widened. "I'll prepare a proper bath. It'll be ready shortly."

"Thank you, Gosuk Ran, but we don't have time. Besides, Fasanzoerl take Guzas all the time."

"Really?" For some reason, this boggled the controller. "And what would you like to drink?"

Humming, Lafiel looked to Jinto.

"Surgu, please. Cold." Even though he wasn't thirsty, he was tired, so Jinto placed an order for coffee.

"Teal Nom. Hot, with a slice of Rop," Lafiel decided.

"Gross!" Jinto teased. He stopped chuckling as soon as he noticed the controller glaring at him.

"Very good. I'll bring the Teal Nom at once." With a bow, the controller backed out of the room.

"I wonder if I'll get that Surgu," Jinto mused indifferently.

"I don't like it here," Lafiel announced.

"I couldn't agree more." It bugged Jinto to be ignored. Granted, he was with a member of the Fasanzoerl, but these vassals could have at least acknowledged his existence.

Eventually, the controller returned with another woman and an Onhokia, which came to a stop right beside Jinto.

"Go ahead." The controller continued to glare at Jinto.

"Thank you." Glad at least that he wasn't snubbed, Jinto grabbed the cup of chilled coffee from the Onhokia.

The other woman tentatively brought forth Lafiel's peach juice. Nervously, she approached the table, trembling badly enough to spill a drop or two on the table.

The two women looked at each other as if they'd just been caught leaving a flaming bag of dog crap on the Lartnei's doorstep.

"Now you've done it, Seelnay!"

"I'm so sorry!" Seelnay apologized, bowing all the way to the floor.

Amazed, Jinto couldn't figure out why they were so upset. *It's just a drop!*

Lafiel was equally dumbstruck. "What's wrong?"

"I spilled the drink offered to Feia Lartneir. Please forgive this rude act."

"Rude act?" Lafiel looked at the droplets on the table. "There's no need to apologize. See?" She wiped up the spill with her finger, eliciting a scream from Seelnay.

"Oh! I'm not worthy!" Seelnay pointed to Lafiel's finger. "I'll clean it up right away!"

"Never mind." Lafiel lowered her hand. "It's okay, really. I have a napkin here."

Seelnay was nearly in tears. Lafiel looked to Jinto for help. "Um," Jinto thought fast, "if you keep apologizing, it *will* eventually become rude. So, please stop."

"Y-yes." Seelnay bit her lip and bowed.

"Excuse us for now," said the controller.

"Yes." Seelnay bowed yet again as they left.

"It just gets more and more uncomfortable," Lafiel muttered.

"Are all citizens like that?"

"No. When I was a child, Lef used to scold me a lot."

"And they knew who you were?"

"Of course! They worked in my home."

"You mean Lartei Kryb?"

"Yes. For example, one time, the Lartei gardener gave me an earful after I let the Jazria run wild in the dining room. It ruined a thicket."

"Wait. Why was a mobile pedestal outside? Or why was there thicket inside?"

"No, it's a garden-style dining room."

"Oh." Jinto nodded.

For the most part, Abh lived in artificial environments. They chose when it rained, when it snowed, when the seasons changed, etc. There was no distinction between indoors and outdoors, so they often had flowers in their bedrooms. Thicket in the dining room wasn't unusual at all, apparently.

Lafiel continued her story.

After he saw the floral carnage, the gardener had respectfully told the Lartnei that he took pride in his work and that now the artistic sensibility of the thicket was ruined. He was so upset, he'd said that human beings had not yet invented a suitable way to express it.

After he finished his diatribe, Lafiel apologized, and promised not to do something so stupid in the future.

The gardener, still pretty pissed, said, "If Feia Lartneir's Jazria ever destroys my work again, I guarantee her the opportunity to cultivate an intimate relationship with soil-improvement earthworms!" Then he left.

"After that, my father also scolded me. 'The gardener will be less forgiving if this happens again, and I can't say I blame him. A person's pride is never cheap.' "

"But the gardner was the exception, right?"

"No! The Kryb and the nobles' vassals who knew me were all just as proud of their work."

"Okay." Jinto was finally convinced. "Well, the women here seem pretty proud to me."

"You're just saying that because they're ignoring you."

Jinto smirked. "They are? I hadn't noticed."

"I don't like it here. Maybe I'd better give up on a bath."

The stars and fish projected on the wall suddenly cut away. An image of a man appeared. He was Abh, with blue-gray hair that masked most of his face except for his tightly-drawn mouth.

"Excuse my interruption," he greeted them. "I understand you're Feia Lafiel of Lartei Kryb?"

"Yes. I am Abriel Nei-Debrusc Viscountess of Parhynu Lafiel."

"I am Atosrya Syun Atos Lyuf Febdash Klowal. Pleased to meet you."

"Hello, Lyuf." Lafiel nodded, then pointed to Jinto. "This is Linn Syun-Rock Jarluk Dreu Haider Jinto Lonyu."

"Hello, Lonyu Lyum." Jinto bowed slightly.

"Pleased to meet you, Lonyu Jarluk Dreu." Now that they'd exchanged pleasantries, the baron immediately turned his full attention to Lafiel.

"I must apologize, Feia Lartneir."

"For what?" Lafiel asked warily.

"Truthfully . . . oh, this is awkward . . . we've determined that we don't have sufficient fuel to meet your needs."

"How can that be? Your Belysega—"

"That's where the awkwardness comes in. The Space Traffic Control personnel made a mistake. My apologies."

"Fine. Then can you supply me directly from a fuel tank asteroid?"

"Don't be ridiculous," Lyuf Febdak said, slightly amused.

For reasons unknown, Jinto shuddered.

"Feia Lartneir has finally come here," the baron continued, "and it would bring great shame on the Lyumjhe Febdak to let you leave like this. Please, by all means, allow me to ferry you to my humble Garish."

"Thank you for the invitation," Lafiel knitted her brow, "but we're on a military mission, so I have no time to make myself at home. Haven't you heard the news? If not, ask your Gosuk. This isn't a courtesy call, Lyuf."

"Of course I've heard, Feia. But I must insist."

"Again, that's very kind. However," she was clearly losing patience, "if you know the news, perhaps you have better things to do than welcome us. For instance, maybe you should withdraw from your Skor?"

"It's nice of you to be concerned, but we don't have Menyu. There's nothing we can do."

"Even so—"

"Here's the deal," the baron interrupted. "All the Sov Vekekar are in a very distant orbit. There are only empty asteroids nearby."

"That's absurd!"

"You don't believe me, Feia?" The baron grimaced. "I think I know my own business."

"Forgive me," Lafiel apologized meekly. "Even if they're far away, we must get to them at once."

"Already taken care of. I'm arranging an asteroid to arrive in about twelve hours."

"Twelve hours!" Lafiel hollered.

The baron smiled. "Therefore, Feia, please accept my invitation in the meantime. In my Garish, you can get cleaned up, and I will offer you a meal. I have military experience; I know what it's like on the inside of a Pelia. I can't imagine a member of the Fasanzoerl spending such a long time in such an uncomfortable environment."

"I'm not Fasanzoerl now," Lafiel reminded him. "I'm here as a Labule officer."

The baron folded his hands. "Then, as Fapyut, I request more detailed information from the Labule. I'm entitled to that, am I not?"

"Oh," Lafiel said, trapped. No way around that request. "That's right, Lyuf. I forgot. The Resii *Gosroth's* logbook is on this ship, so I'll get you a copy of the pertinent information."

"Very good," the baron said discontentedly. "I will keep a seat for you at dinner."

Listening to this conversation made Jinto nervous. *Is this always how Frybar upper classes spoke?*

Lafiel was much more formal than she was when speaking with Jinto, which he supposed made sense, but it still felt like an argument.

"We'll arrive faster if we take the Pelia to meet the fuel tank asteroid. I want to depart at once, after we hand over a copy of the log," Lafiel insisted.

"Exactly," the baron confirmed. "But I've received word that Feia's Pelia needs to be inspected. You can't leave quite yet."

"Inspected?" Lafiel repeated, shocked.

"Yes. I don't know the details—you'll have to ask our mechanic. She's busy right now, so just relax for a moment." The baron spoke in a strained tone. "A vassal will arrive shortly to guide you. Please wait there."

The image disappeared.

Lafiel glared. "He ignored you, too."

"A little bit." The whole conversation had taken place as if Jinto didn't exist. "I guess it can't be helped. When there's a Fasanzoerl and a simple nobleman involved, of course he's going to pay more attention to the Fasanzoerl."

"If he really wanted to welcome me, he would have invited you, too, right?"

"Yeah." Jinto thought about the conversation. From an outside perspective, the baron had definitely been rude. Sadly, however, Jinto was accustomed to rude treatment, so he wasn't particularly offended. "Thanks for being outraged on my behalf."

"Oh, I'm not mad on your account."

"Oh." Jinto sipped his coffee.

"I don't trust him. The Pelia needs *inspection?* Come on. I don't think a small Skor like this even has the technological capability to do that! Maybe he just wants to detain us."

"Why would he do that? You're being paranoid, Lafiel."

"I told you, I don't trust him. I don't *like* him."

"Can't argue with you there." Jinto crossed his arms. *If Lyuf Febdak were the first Abh I met, instead of Lafiel or Lexshu, I doubt I would have ever become friends with any Abh.*

Maybe the baron would become more tolerable or even friendly over time.

"Think about it logically for a minute. If Lonyu Lyum has a plot in mind, what could it be? What could he possibly gain by keeping us here?" Jinto asked.

Deep in thought, Lafiel tilted her head.

"Maybe he wants the Pelia," Jinto suggested.

"Why?"

"Duh. To escape from the enemy fleet!"

"The Pelia only has two seats, so only two people could escape."

He shrugged. "If the baron plans to escape by himself, two seats would be plenty."

"And abandon his Gosuk?"

"So you don't trust the baron, but you think he'd be honorable enough to stay with them?"

"Onyu!" she cried. "It has nothing to do with individual ethics. Abandoning vassals or Sos is the most shameful act a noble can commit. Rue Razem would never forgive him that. Plus, if he stole a military vessel . . . Well, he'd be better off in a United Mankind prison camp than facing that kind of Frybar punishment."

"Ah, so Sune comes with Slymekoth."

"Yes, military service is required of all those with court rank," Lafiel assented.

"On the other hand," Jinto just couldn't keep his opinion to himself, "when people are at their wits' end, you never know what they'll do, right? When I was in Dreuhynu Vorlak, I heard a story once about a high-rise that caught fire. Some of the people trapped on the thirty-fifth floor chose to jump. I guess they preferred falling to burning. Maybe the Lyuf doesn't like fire."

"Did he look like a person at his wits' end to you?"

"I guess not. But that doesn't necessarily mean he's up to something."

"True."

"Okay. If he welcomes us, I'll go too, and keep an eye on you."

As Lafiel rolled her eyes, she caught a glimpse of the baron's Gosuk approaching.

The bath felt great.

Soaking in a tub of hot water, Lafiel felt cleansed of more than just sweat and grime. *What a relief!*

However, she could not be a hundred percent at ease, because she was not alone.

The woman named Seelnay had accompanied her into the bathroom (Gorv), trying hard to help Lafiel. "Please, I'll wash your back," she kept saying, and, "Please, I'll wash your hair."

Ever since she was capable, Lafiel had washed herself. *People have the craziest notions about the life of the Fasanzoerl.*

Despite Lafiel's protests, Seelnay would not believe that Feia Lartnei knew how to use liquid soap (Satyrl).

"Please, don't be shy!"

Shy! Is she serious? Lafiel wondered. Finally, she got fed up and just gave in.

Seelnay waited next to the bath with a fluffy white bathrobe (Gusath).

"Did you know that an enemy fleet is heading toward Loebehynu Sufagnaum?" Lafiel asked, nearly submerged.

"Yes."

"Aren't you afraid?"

"No. My master, the Fal Sif, will take care of it. He takes care of everything."

"The Lyuf? You trust him?" she asked the young woman.

"Of course! If it weren't for him, I wouldn't even be here now!"

"What do you mean?"

"Ever since I was a little girl, I wanted to be a Lef. But I didn't want to join the military, and I definitely didn't have the technical skill to be a vassal."

"If you wanted it for so long," Lafiel pointed out, "you should have had time to get an education."

"In my homeland, Dreuhynu Friizal, women aren't allowed to get a Gosuk-level education. We're really only expected to be good wives and mothers in Friiza. I used to think all Nahen were like that, until I learned better."

"Really?"

"Yes. Fal Sif picked me up from that world and gave me an education."

"Is that so?" *What kind of education does a person need to wash others' backs?*

"Yes. I have learned enough to be in charge of adjustment and inspection of any antimatter fuel tanks."

"Oh, so you're not a Gorv specialist?"

"No. It's the first time I've served in a Gorv. I've never been summoned to the master's bath."

"Does another vassal wash the Lyuf's back?"

She frowned. "Well, he can't reach it himself."

This Lyumusko is nuts! Lafiel concluded. Most of the time, the most personal of vassal duties was being a waiter at meals. Attending to a sovereign in the Gorv seemed excessive.

"He is a very kind master," Seelnay said fondly.

"That doesn't make him a good leader," Lafiel sniped.

The attendant shrugged. "What can I do, other than keep faith in my lord?"

Quickly changing the subject, Lafiel asked how many people were in the Ribeun.

"Probably about fifty. But nobody's conducted a census. If you really want to know, you should ask —"

"How many are Abh?" Lafiel interrupted.

"Two. My lord and his father. Apparently, he has a younger sister, but she's been on Lakfakalle for a long time."

"Sounds lonely."

"True," Seelnay agreed. "There isn't much excitement here, but we're accustomed to it, so it doesn't bother us much."

Looking down at her pruny fingers, Lafiel decided it was an opportune time to get out of the bath. *If I soak any longer, I'm going to suffer water damage.* She stood up.

"Beautiful!" sighed Seelnay, staring at Lafiel's perfectly-proportioned limbs and smooth skin.

As a rule, Lafiel did not value compliments on her looks, which were entirely the result of genetic engineering instead of any personal accomplishment. But she let it go.

Gingerly, Seelnay wrapped the Lartnei in the Gusath.

Seelnay bowed as Lafiel left. Upon exiting the room, an older Gosuk presented her with a plethora of robes and bath towels.

Disgusted, Lafiel asked whether the mansion had a body dryer.

"Our master says those are barbaric devices," the older Gosuk replied, wrapping Lafiel's hair in a towel. Seelnay exchanged the wet Gusath for a new, dry one.

Once Lafiel resigned herself to it, the pampering actually felt pretty good.

I hope Jinto's getting the VIP treatment too, she thought. *Hey, I wonder if there are any male vassals?* She couldn't say why, but Lafiel certainly hoped so. For some reason, she didn't like the idea of Jinto naked in front of other girls.

Satisfied that she was thoroughly dried, the Gosuk led Lafiel to some clothes that had already been laid out. There was a daffodil-colored robe that was garnished with rubies, diamonds, and cat's-eyes resting beside a tasteful green Sorf. These clothes were fit for a palace.

"What happened to my Serlin?" Lafiel asked.

"We're washing your uniform now," the older vassal answered.

"Not by hand, I hope," Lafiel said, only half joking. It shouldn't take longer than her bath.

"Master said a Serlin at a dinner party is too . . . um, well . . . stiff."

"Too stiff?"

He's got a lot of nerve, Lafiel thought, *thinking he can play dress-up doll with me!* "I will only wear my Serlin," she declared. "If it's being washed, then I will wait here until it's done."

"But . . ." On the verge of tears, the older vassal's face wrinkled up.

"Please, Feia Lartneir," Seelnay pleaded, practically pressing her nose into the floor.

Lafiel felt ridiculous. But she also felt sorry for these women. "Okay," Lafiel compromised, "I'll wear the robe over my Serlin. How's that?"

The two Gosuk exchanged looks. "Well . . . we can't disobey Feia Lartneir!"

Is it really that big a deal? While the vassals continued to fret quietly, Lafiel's thoughts turned to the *Gosroth*, somewhere far away, fighting the enemy, while she argued about what to wear to dinner. Suddenly her problems seemed a lot less important. *The battle's probably already over. I hope we were victorious.*

"Very well, Feia." They had reached a conclusion. "We'll bring your Serlin at once."

I guess they're done washing it, after all.

The older vassal returned shortly with the Serlin, then picked up Lafiel's undergarments. "Please put these on before you catch a cold."

As if trimming a tree, the two women dressed Lafiel.

"You're very efficient," Lafiel marveled.

"We're very experienced," the older vassal said.

"Oh? Do you always do this kind of thing?"

"Yes. Don't you have servants, Feia?" the Gosuk asked incredulously.

"We have chamberlains, but nothing like this."

"You're kidding." She actually didn't believe it.

After the clothes were all in place, Seelnay brought a tray. "Your ornaments."

A blinding assembly of precious metals and jewels were placed before Lafiel.

"Please choose whatever you like, Feia Lartneir," the older Gosuk said.

Lafiel squinted enough to see what was missing. "What happened to my Alpha and Kreuno?"

"Those barbaric things?"

Lafiel frowned. "They're essential, not barbaric."

Even though she knew these women were simply doing as they were told, Lafiel couldn't help getting angry. *Do they honestly not know the functions of the Kreuno and tiara?*

The Kreuno contained her electromagnetic family crest and individual data. And the diadem on the silk-lined tray, while lovely, could not assist Frokaj like the Alpha.

"Understood, Feia. As you wish." The older Gosuk sighed, nodding to Seelnay.

Seelnay practically ran to retrieve the tiara and wrist device.

A few minutes later, as she placed the Alpha on her head and her Frokaj was returned, Lafiel felt like someone emerging from a long, pitch-black tunnel.

The vassal took Lafiel straight from the bathroom to the dining hall (called the Bisiaf), which had a pale blue floor and a ceiling speckled with stars. The holographic fish swam on every surface of this room.

Lafiel could not take her eyes off what was, quite possibly, the ugliest-looking fish in the universe.

The baron sure has horrible taste, she concluded.

Lafiel wandered toward the dining table in the center of the room, which was small enough to make the chamber seem overly large.

Lyuf Febdak waited at the table. A scantily-clad female Gosuk stood behind his chair. The food wasn't on the table yet, just two amethyst wine glasses (Lamteysh).

In customary fashion, the Lyuf stood and bowed his head.

Lafiel stopped in her tracks. "Where's Jinto?"

"Jinto?" The baron looked confused. "Oh! You mean Lonyu Jarluk Dreu Haider? The Lonyu is with my father."

"They aren't dining with us?"

"No. My father hates people."

Lafiel cocked her head. "Then why is he with Jinto?"

The baron sported a mysterious expression. "Misery loves company."

"What does that mean?"

"Forget it."

"Too late. Besides, it is my duty to take Jinto—I mean Jarluk Dreu Haider—to Sufagnaum."

"Please, Feia." Lyuf raised an eyebrow. "He's fine. You don't think I'd let anything happen to Lonyu Jarluk Dreu, do you?"

Lafiel crossed her arms. "You are acting very suspiciously."

"How regrettable!" the baron exclaimed nonchalantly. "At any rate, take a seat. Maybe I can clear up your misconceptions over dinner?"

"I hope it *is* just a misunderstanding, Lyuf."

The waitress pulled a chair out for Lafiel. She sat, and the baron followed suit.

"Can I offer you a drink?" he asked.

"Anything without Skiade is fine. I'm still on duty."

"As you wish. Is Tyl Lashuban okay?"

Lafiel nodded, and the baron snapped his fingers.

"Feia Lartneir, I noticed you called that boy," his nose wrinkled ever so slightly, "by name. Please, call me Klowal."

"I can't do that."

"Why not?"

"Because I don't want to, Lyuf."

Falling silent, the baron glared at Lafiel.

Temporarily breaking the increasing tension, the female Gosuk returned with a jar on a tray. Carefully, the waitress picked up the jar and filled Lafiel's Lamteysh halfway with mandarin orange juice. Then she proceeded to fill the baron's Lamteysh nearly to the brim with Rinmo.

Thirsty after her long bath, Lafiel downed the juice in one gulp. Without missing a beat, the waitress refilled it.

The baron and Lafiel were ominously silent as hors d'oeuvres made their way to the table. Classically Abh, the presentation of the food was as impressive as its flavor. Pale flower petals adorned the tidy, black tray.

"Please, help yourself."

"Don't mind if I do." With her silver Grei, Lafiel grabbed what she thought was a tree leaf. Popping it into her mouth, Lafiel was surprised to find that it was actually some kind of shellfish. "That's good."

"I'm honored, Feia."

"That's praise for the cook," Lafiel said, rather rudely, "not you. I assume it's made by a person, not a machine."

"Good guess, Feia. I'm not big on machines." A pause. "You seem to be angry about something."

"Yes, Lyuf. I am angry."

"Is my company really so terrible?"

As she deftly picked up a Riopos (a smoked thigh bone shaped like an iris flower), she looked sharply at the baron. "You're certainly not explaining the misunderstanding."

"About that lander boy?"

"Jinto is Bar Sif—*Abh* nobility."

The baron smiled. "Good for him."

"Call me crazy, Baron, but I'm starting to think my Pelia didn't need to be inspected at all. And maybe, just maybe, there's more fuel here than you say."

"You got me. I lied." The baron spoke frankly. "There's plenty of fuel. Your Pelia is fine."

Lafiel wasn't entirely surprised. She pushed the now-empty hors d'oeuvres tray aside. "So, why did you lie to me, Baron?"

"Because no matter how nicely I asked, Feia Lartneir wouldn't come to my dinner party."

"I'm on a *mission*."

"Then it's good that I lied."

She glared. "I hate being deceived, Baron."

"I'm sure you do." He smiled.

"Then you'll understand that I must leave at once."

"About that . . ." The Lyuf slurped his cider, "I'm afraid I have to keep you around a little longer."

"That is not an option."

The waitress brought a tray of bowls containing Orton Fimferma. Lafiel removed the lid and rejoiced in the aroma of freshly steamed sea turtle flippers.

"I can't let you go. I'll use force if I have to, but you're going to stay." The baron continued to speak while sporting a smile.

"For how long?"

"Until the next Frybar ship comes, and the safety of my Skor is assured."

"But who knows how long that will be?" she asked, a slight edge to her voice. But she remained calm. As long as she was there, she decided to eat the soup.

"Indeed."

Bewildered, Lafiel frowned. She wasn't as angry as she thought she should be. *What does the Lyuf have up his sleeve?*

"If it means anything to you, I'm not planning to commit treason," announced the baron.

"No—you're not brave enough to be a traitor."

An eerie smirk on his face, the baron nodded. "I think it's genetic; I'm not prone to bravery."

Ignoring the baron for the time being, Lafiel ate her soup. When she finally did look up at him, she noticed he'd hardly touched his food.

Did he drug me? she wondered. *No, that's simply ridiculous. If he wanted to do that, I would have felt it right after the hors d'oeuvres. And he wouldn't have put it into his own food as well!*

After Lafiel's soup was gone, a tray of trout wrapped in balls of rice (Dersluf Bos) was brought to the table. The fish was genetically engineered to fit into the miniature rice balls.

"So?" Lafiel pressed as she peeled the wheat baking-cloth off one of the fish. "Why are you keeping us here? Is it some kind of personal grudge?"

"Don't be silly! As long as Feia Lartneir is in this house, I intend to show you the warmest of welcomes. Your presence can only add to the splendor of this household."

"I'm not sure you've grasped the seriousness of your actions here."

"I understand completely; I'm protecting my Skor."

She swallowed. "How does detaining us possibly equate to protecting your Ribeun?"

"Loebehynu Sufagnaum is a big star system." The Lyuf spread his arms for emphasis. "So of course the United Mankind knows how to find it. My Lyumusko, however, is only about this big." He scrunched up his face and brought his index finger to his thumb.

"Thus, it's quite likely the United Mankind doesn't even know that Lyumusko Febdak exists. And if they don't know, I'm not about to tell them. But if they saw your little ship zipping in and out of Sord Febdak, they'd probably investigate, and I can't have that. Worst case, they could attack us, unprovoked."

"We already passed through Sord Febdak. How do you know they didn't notice then?"

"They might have, but I'm not going to double their chances of locating this Skor by letting you go back through."

"I see."

Nodding emphatically, the baron continued. "Therefore, Feia Lartneir, although you'd like to leave, I cannot let you do that until the enemy has cleared the area.

If the enemy fleet gets destroyed, you won't have to wait very long. On the other hand, if they are victorious, you'll have to wait until the Frybar can win back this territory."

"Can you survive here that long?"

"We've got Glaik and agricultural lands. We'll be fine. Although the food we can produce with our limited resources may be slightly less refined than what you're accustomed to eating."

"What will you do if this zone is never recovered?"

He paused. "Cross that bridge when we come to it. The lord of this small Skor can only deal with so much at a time."

"Maybe you should think a little further into the future." Lafiel picked at her fish absentmindedly.

"Why do you say that?"

"You're obstructing the passage of a military Pelia. The Frybar might see that as grounds to take away your Ribeun, even after you've gone to such great lengths to save it."

"That won't happen. The Skas Lazasot will deem my conduct suitable to the situation; everything I've done was out of devotion to protecting the Skor. At the very worst, I'll have to pay a fine."

"Have you considered the fact that, as a result of your devotion, Loebehynu Sufagnaum will receive no warning of an imminent attack? Do you think the Skas Lazasot is really going to look the other way on that one?"

"Shouldn't be a problem. There's enough traffic in the area that someone else will surely report the enemy fleet. There's nothing wrong with what I've done. In a court of law, could you deny that I've treated you well? On the name of Abriel?"

"Until I grant you permission to say my family name," Lafiel smoldered, "don't."

"Fair enough." The Lyuf bowed halfheartedly. "Please forgive me, Feia."

Pushing aside the half-eaten rice ball, Lafiel cleared her throat. Another waitress, a Batia, cleared away her dishes.

"Where's Jinto?"

"I've given him a lander's welcome."

"How many times do I have to tell you?" Lafiel scolded him. "Jinto is Imperial nobility. Besides, I'm not sure I like your idea of lander status. I've never seen anyone as servile as the Gosuk here. They're like circus animals doing tricks for peanuts! It's pathetic." Lafiel half hoped the waitress overheard.

"The relationship between a sovereign and his vassal is nobody else's business, not even for the Spunej Erumita."

"Maybe so, but it just makes me wonder what you'd consider a suitable 'lander's welcome.' "

"You've nothing to worry about, Feia Lartneir," the Lyuf said stubbornly.

A dish of boiled pumpkin stuffed with meat and vegetables was placed before her. *The food just keeps coming!* Lafiel had to admit it was delicious.

Staring at the vermilion Skalish with the pumpkin on it, Lafiel addressed the baron. "Listen, Lyuf. Just as you have a Skor to protect, I have a mission. Mine is to deliver Jinto safely to Safugnoff. If something happens to him, you'd better pray that Skas Lazasot gives you a quick death."

"What's so special about that lander? I certainly don't see the appeal."

"If you were in the military," Lafiel glared, "you would understand the sanctity of duty. This is my first military mission, and I intend to carry it out even if that means condemning your precious Skor to a fiery grave."

"I just can't allow that." The baron remained calm, at least externally.

After two or three bites of pumpkin, Lafiel stood up.

The waitress seemed confused. "Please, Feia, it is merely a break between courses. There is more to come!"

"I've had enough. My thanks and apologies to the chef — the food was very delicious."

Clapping, the Lyuf demanded that someone guide Feia Lartneir to her bedroom. "Feia is tired," the baron said creepily. "Please wait with her until she's gone to sleep."

So that's how it's going to be, is it? Lafiel sighed. "Just curious, Baron. Do you have any male Gosuk?"

"No. I can't stand being in the same room as lander men."

A huge smile appeared on Lafiel's face.

People who feared or hated the Abh postulated that the Abh only *really* smiled at inappropriate times. Although this theory seemed absurd, it was based on an interesting Abh mannerism — they also smiled to indicate loathing.

Known as "the Abh smile," the expression resembled a suppressed laugh with a twist of defiance, but it was entirely too gruesome to be called derision. Like a bouquet of scorched roses, there's no way someone could mistake it for a display of affection.

"The number of reasons I have to hate you," Lafiel said with an Abh smile on her lips, "has just increased by one."

Where am I? When he woke up, Jinto's entire body felt heavy, like all his blood had been replaced with mud.

Opening his eyes to a wooden wall that was decorated with a three-dimensional carving of ivy, Jinto realized he was on a hard bed.

Memories oozed sluggishly through his mind.

The last thing he remembered, someone was supposed to take him to a Gorv. He had parted with Lafiel after arriving at the main building and coming through the corridor from the spaceport. Of course, they couldn't use the same Gorv. That made sense. What *didn't* make sense was why somebody used a pressure injector to juice him with sedatives immediately after Lafiel left.

Even though it had to be a Gosuk who'd doped Jinto, the orders must have come from Lyuf Febdak.

That weasel!

Even more worried about Lafiel than he was angry with the Lyuf, Jinto sprang to his feet.

"Oh, Faneb, you're awake!" someone said directly beside him. Jinto was surprised to see that the friendly voice calling him "young man" belonged to an elderly gentleman dressed in the long robe of a noble. With his snow-white hair, he looked at least seventy, maybe older, but very stout and healthy.

"Who are you?"

"It's really more polite to introduce yourself before asking."

True enough. "I'm Linn Syun-Rock Jarluk Dreu Haider Jinto."

"A count? Ho! You don't look Abh."

"Neither do you," Jinto shot back.

"Well, we *are* the same species. I'm Atosryua Syun Atos Lyuf Raika Febdak Srguf. I was the second Lyuf Febdak."

"You're the former baron? And the current Lyuf is . . . ?"

"My son."

"Well, what do you want with me?" Jinto asked angrily.

"Me? I'm just an old man, concerned with the well-being of an unconscious young fellow. But I guess you're okay now."

Raising his voice, Jinto said, "Don't you play dumb with me!"

"Calm down, Faneb. I assure you, although my son seems to have something in the works, I don't have the foggiest what it could be. I'm a prisoner here, too."

"Prisoner?" Jinto echoed, confused.

"More or less. Don't get me wrong—I live very comfortably; I'm just not allowed to go anywhere. What would you call that?"

"Tell me this, then. Is Lafiel here? I mean, was I the only one brought in, or was there also a girl?"

"Girl? No, it was just you. Why? Is she your lover?"

Jinto was too busy looking at his bare wrist to humor the old man. "Where's my Kreuno?"

"Who knows? If it's not here, my son probably took it."

"You really don't know anything?" Jinto pressed.

"Sorry." The old man shrugged again. "They never tell me anything."

"But the Lonyu Lyum is your son."

"Maybe that's *why*. I think he's ashamed to have a lander for a father. That's why he keeps me here, where no one will see me."

"It just gets more and more confusing." Rubbing his still-throbbing temples, Jinto realized that he wasn't wearing his Alpha. He looked down—the symbol of his noble status wasn't on his Daush. But these were minor concerns compared to the missing Kreuno.

"Maybe he's got one of those inferiority complexes," the old man offered.

"That's not the impression I got."

"Well I'm his father, so I'd know better than you. Lyumjhe Febdak has almost no ancestral history. He can't stand it." The poor old guy shook his head.

"But he's Imperial nobility. He has a Skor."

"A really tiny Skor!"

"Tiny or not, it's still a big deal, right?" Jinto asked.

"It is a high social standing, but we were just Lef until three generations ago. He detests that fact. You know, he didn't just shut me in here so that other people wouldn't see me—*he's* the one who couldn't stand to see his lander father."

"You don't seem much like a lander to me."

The Lyuf Raika grinned. "I've had a lot of time to think about the mistakes I've made raising my son. You should consult me when you're ready to have a kid."

"Um . . . Maybe later." Jinto felt way too young to even *think* about having a child. "Right now, we should concentrate on getting out of here."

Jinto tried to get off the bed, but his legs didn't want to cooperate. He fell over; probably an aftereffect of the drug.

"Don't overdo it, Lonyu Jarluk Dreu," the former baron said, catching him.

"Please, don't be so formal. It makes me nervous."

"You've got all kinds of problems, don't you, Faneb?"

"Yes." Jinto trembled slightly.

"But you *are* a Dreu, huh? Isn't that a Voda rank? Whichever member of your family went from being a Lef to a Sif deserves a round of applause—that's no easy feat."

"It's my father. He wasn't even Rue Lef, so he did quite well for himself."

"That sounds like a good story. Care to share?"

Jinto huffed. "No, not particularly."

"Fine, spoilsport. Oh jeez! Now I *really* want to know! Oh well, I must respect your wishes. How about a Guzas? You look like you could use one."

Jinto would have loved a shower, but there wasn't time. "Thanks, but later. We have to escape quickly."

"I think you should rest first. Get cleaned up, have some food. Get some of the strength back in those legs. Then we can address all your problems."

Although this easygoing old man seemed trustworthy, Jinto was reluctant to take his outstretched hand. *Even if the old guy actually intends to help me, will he be able to accomplish anything? After all, he keeps saying that he is a prisoner.*

"Trust an old man," the baron assured him. "At least go and dunk yourself in the water for a few seconds."

The concept of time suddenly came back to Jinto "But there's no time! How long was I out?"

The old man squinted at his Kreuno. "Must be about five hours. See, one or two more hours won't hurt."

Five hours?!

There was still enough time to outrun the enemy fleet. But where was Lafiel? Five hours was more than enough time to subject a Feia to the most heinous of plans.

"Could I use your Kreuno for a second?" Always prepared, Jinto had memorized Lafiel's Kreuno number in case of emergency. If she wore hers, and was anywhere within a lightsecond, he would be able to contact her.

"Sure." The Lyuf Raika took off his Kreuno and handed it over. "I can't figure out how to work the damn thing anyway."

Jinto looked at the Kreuno. It was just a wristwatch. He sighed and handed it back.

"Does this place have a Luode?"

"Yes."

"Can I use that?" Jinto asked impatiently.

"Be my guest, but I should warn you that it will only work in the Banzorl Garyuk. So if you're trying to talk to that girl, she'd have to be in a specific household room."

Jinto slumped onto the bed.

"Now quit being a party pooper and go to the Gorv," the former baron said, the same way a parent tells a kid to quit picking his nose. "Clear your head. Eat some food. Maybe then we can come up with a plan."

"Fine." Jinto caved in, deciding he might need to regain his strength.

Pushing aside the soft, warm blanket, Lafiel sprang to her feet. Completely contrary to Jinto's drug-induced grogginess, Lafiel felt refreshed and clearheaded after her nap. Despite resting only a short time, she felt strong.

"Lights," she commanded quietly. Lafiel was relieved to see that she was alone.

Per the baron's request, two Gosuk had stayed with her until she fell asleep. At first she tried to feign sleep, but when she closed her eyes, she must have been more tired than she thought, because she quickly fell into a heavy slumber.

Checking her Kreuno, Lafiel determined she had been asleep for almost four hours. *Just like a kid*, Lafiel chastised herself, *pretending to fall asleep, then actually sleeping*.

Thinking about the Lyuf and his plot, she quickly grew infuriated. Through the eyes of someone used to getting her own way, the baron seemed extremely unreasonable and stubborn. And on top of that, his pigheadedness impeded her first military mission.

Even though I'm an Abriel, Imperial Wrath incarnate, I'm very patient, Lafiel assessed. *But I have limits*.

She would escape just to teach the baron a lesson.

Opening the clothesbasket (Rawarf), she found her Serlin among other more spectacular garments. She didn't even look twice at them. There would be time for plenty of gorgeous clothes later, when the Lartnei returned to the Flirish.

It's weird that the Lyuf has so much clothing suitable for an Imperial princess, Lafiel thought, *when there aren't any Abh women in the Lyumex*.

Lafiel put on her Serlin. *I wonder where Jinto is*.

She fired up her Kreuno and attempted to contact Jinto's Kreuno.

"I'm sorry. The Kreuno you've requested is not being worn. Please disconnect and try your call again later. If you feel you've reached this message in error—"

"Humph." Lafiel shut it off. Of course the Lyuf didn't want her to communicate with Jinto. Ever resourceful, Lafiel started up the Soteyua in the bedroom. Once it booted up, she located an internal map of the house.

The Lyumex had three floors, which were partitioned into living areas, business areas, storage, water factories, farmable land, and so on.

"Display current location," Lafiel ordered the terminal.

The display zoomed in on the floor plan for Level Three, revealing a dot in one of the rooms near the center.

"Show me the Lyuf's bedroom."

It was right next door.

"The guest bedrooms?"

About twenty different rooms lit up.

"Of those, which are occupied?"

Only one stayed red; the room Lafiel was in.

"Are there any prisoners in the Lyumex?"

"I don't understand the question." The computer was smart, but it wasn't *that* smart.

"Show me the names and locations of all the people currently in this house."

"That operation requires Fal Sif's permission. He is resting and could not grant permission until morning."

Even the computer calls him master. "Never mind."

At this rate, I'd be better off just asking the Lyuf! Lafiel regretted leaving her weapon on the Pelia, but the baron surely would have taken it from her, anyway. *Maybe I'll just go get it now.*

It was the middle of the night; Lafiel doubted she would run into a vassal in the hallway. She knew where the Pelia was. The only problem was getting to it.

"Can I enter the spaceport? Does a pressurized corridor exist between here and the docked Pelia?"

"It exists."

"Is it sealed?" she asked.

"No, but a Saij Daifat Heita is required to pass through."

An electromagnectic wave family crest key? "Is my Defath registered?"

"No, your ID does not register."

Lafiel sighed. "Can I register it now?"

"That operation requires Fal Sif's permission. He is resting and could not grant permission—"

"Whose Defath *are* registered?" Lafiel interrupted.

"Fal Sif and all of the Gosuk. The full names of the Gosuk are—"

"That's enough, thanks." Lafiel stopped the machine. *I'll just have to try my luck.*

The circumstances were less than ideal . . . but she couldn't just sit in the bedroom forever. She downloaded the map of the house into her Kreuno. *Preparations complete.*

Lafiel went to the door, but stopped just short of leaving. Something was wrong, but she couldn't put her finger on it. Warily, Lafiel rebooted the terminal.

"Is the Lyuf's father here?"

"Yes, Lonyu Lyum Raika lives in Lyumex Febdak."

"And his Defath isn't registered?"

"No. It is not."

"Why not?"

"Fal Sif's orders."

"Why did he order that?"

"That operation requires Fal Sif's—"

"Okay, okay. I get the picture." Lafiel had little patience with automated Soteyua. "Where is Lyuf Raika's residence?"

Again, the map of the third floor popped up, zeroing in on a corridor that ran alongside a pasture and a water plant. At the end, there was an isolated residential area, which lit up.

"I want to meet with Lonyu Lyum Raika. Make an appointment."

"That operation—"

"No!" Lafiel smacked the table. "I do not want to ask permission! Why do I need the Lyuf's permission to meet with Lyuf Raika? Doesn't that seem weird to you?"

"I cannot evaluate 'weird.' "

Lafiel had a couple of un-Lartnei-like words for the computer terminal. "Is there anybody else in the area of Lyuf Raika?"

"Yes. There is one other person."

"Who?"

"No data."

"Is it a vassal?"

"No."

Jackpot! That must be where Jinto is.

"I'd probably need an ID to go to the Lyuf Raika's room, huh?"

"You need an electromagnetic wave family crest. That operation also requires Fal Sif's permission. He is—"

"Don't even say it!" Dejected, Lafiel cursed the machine. She hadn't felt so aggravated since her last encounter with an Onwarele!

Apparently, the baron and his father had some kind of screwed-up relationship. Lafiel wasn't surprised; this was not uncommon in a noble family.

Opening the clothesbasket, Lafiel looked around for a long robe, thinking it might facilitate concealing a weapon. Fianlly, she settled on a crimson Daush that was embroidered with a silver bird.

She went into the corridor.

"Feia Lartneir!"

Busted.

A Gosuk stood from an uncomfortable-looking chair and bowed.

"Seelnay, right?"

"Yes! It's an honor, Feia Lartneir," she nearly swooned, "for you to remember the name of a humble servant like me!"

Please stop gushing, Lafiel thought. She didn't want to interfere with another family's Jhedirl, but this was getting ridiculous. The Lyuf's Gosuk greatly overshot the necessary degree of servitude.

Plenty of vassals served Lartei Kryb; Lafiel had been surrounded by servants since birth. However, they all knew the difference between sincerity and slavery. All she wanted was to be treated like a normal person; sycophantic Gosuk made Lafiel feel like a pompous ass.

"What are you doing?" Lafiel asked the vassal. "Were you watching me?"

"Of course not." Seelnay's eyes widened. "I would never do such a disrespectful thing. I was waiting for Feia Lartneir to awaken, in case you needed anything."

Lafiel didn't doubt this. If the baron had meant to keep an eye on her, there were easier ways than having someone stand guard outside her door all night.

"Lyuf's orders?"

"While Feia Lartneir stays in this house, I am to attend to you—he told me that."

"Aren't you tired? Don't you need to sleep?"

"Please, please, don't concern yourself. I'll be fine—we take shifts."

"Oh, good," Lafiel said. Lafiel almost felt sorry for her, but Seelnay seemed very content in this environment.

She began to walk, ignoring Seelnay.

"Please wait, Feia Lartneir." Seelnay hurried after Lafiel. "Where are you going?"

"Why?"

"I'll take care of anything you need. Please relax in your room, Feia Lartneir."

"Thanks, but I have to go myself."

"Where are you going?" Seelnay repeated.

"The Pelia." *Why lie?* She couldn't think of a lie fast enough, and Seelnay's wave key might come in handy.

"Oh dear," Seelnay peeped, covering her mouth with her hand. "My deepest apologies, Feia Lartneir, but I must ask you to refrain from entering the Pelia. Fal Sif said—"

"That's funny." Lafiel anticipated that reply. "True, this is the Lyuf's Garish, but the Pelia doesn't belong to the baron. It belongs to the Labule, which has given me permission to pilot the Pelia. So, shouldn't the *Labule* decide who can and can't enter the Pelia?"

"I-I suppose." Seelnay wasn't the brightest bulb in the chandelier. She was used to the baron being the only authority—throwing an opposing power into the mix blew her mind.

They reached the door of the corridor leading to the spaceport—the first barrier Lafiel couldn't pass without using a crest key.

"Won't you open the door? My ID isn't registered," Lafiel said.

Seelnay hesitated. "Feia Lartneir, you put me in a difficult position."

Lafiel didn't say anything; she didn't want the poor girl to tear herself apart, but still . . . Stubbornly determined not to budge, Lafiel just stood, arms folded, staring at the door.

Either Seelnay would let her into the spaceport, or she would have to drag the Lartnei back to the bedroom.

"Feia Lartneir," Seelnay began, "you don't really want to go through with this, do you? You haven't even said goodbye to the baron . . ."

Lafiel had not expected this response. "I'm not leaving. Yet. Don't you know?"

"Know what?" Seelnay reminded Lafiel of a puppy.

"That ship's not going anywhere. The Lyuf refused to give us any fuel. On top of that, he's imprisoned my companion."

Seelnay's mouth dropped open. "Oh, no. Our master couldn't do something like that."

"He did." She stared at the girl. "You really didn't know? The Lyuf must have said something."

"I obey master's orders, but I swear," Seelnay lowered her head, "I didn't know. My understanding was that Feia Lartneir stopped by on break from her military duty."

"You don't know about the enemy fleet's invasion?"

"I've been told that was just a rumor; rumors run rampant in small Skor like this. I only trust reports from the baron."

"Well, now you know. So, what's it going to be?" Lafiel pressed.

"I don't understand." The girl blinked rapidly.

"You are Gosuk Lyum, but you're also Rue Lef. Will you show allegiance to the baron as his vassal, or support my duty as a citizen?"

A long pause. Then, falling to her knees, Seelnay declared she would obey Feia Lartneir's orders.

Lafiel wanted to explain that this wasn't an order from a princess—simply a request from a mere soldier, but then she thought better of it. "I thank you," was all she said.

"But of course." Seelnay stood to open the door.

11 The Former Baron (Lyuf Raika)

The sheer quantity of food made Jinto want to barf. But he had to admit it all tasted delicious.

The meal—chicken and vegetables cooked in a variety of spices—was a welcome change from Abh food, which used little seasoning. At first Jinto had assumed Abh taste buds were different from those of landers. Eventually, he realized that they just preferred subtle flavors. Maybe they found them more elegant or thought them more refined. At any rate, the Lyuf Raika jabbered away with his mouth full of not-so-subtle flavors.

"The first Lyuf Febdak was my mother, but she actually came from an overpopulated Nahen called DiLaplance. Basically, she had to decide whether to move to an emptier world or become Rue Lef."

Jinto nodded and chewed as the old man prattled on.

"Needless to say, she chose the path to Lef, enlisting in the Labule to accelerate the process. She was a Bondev Sashu—infantry. A real badass, my mother. You know about Bondev, boy?"

Swallowing some chicken, Jinto nodded. "It's the department that deals with handheld weapons."

"Very good! In the military, she met a handsome young man. Eventually, they got married and had a really, really beautiful baby."

"Seems like a good thing to do."

"Now, my mother was shrewd, and she was able to weasel her way into Kenru Faziar Robon. You know what that is?"

"Yes, I took the entrance exam to the weapons school."

The Labule's technical system was comprised of four factions. The Faziar Robon planned weapons, the Faziar Har designed ships, the Faziar Sel created engines, and the Faziar Datykirl dealt with computer crystals. Each had an independent Kenru with its own frustratingly difficult entrance exam.

The old man seemed delighted. "Brilliant! After graduating from the weapon design program, she got reassigned to the Faziar Robon, in which she became an officer. After many years as a Sash, she made it to the rank of Lef. So, you could say she did pretty well for herself."

Jinto had to agree. "Yes, that's great."

"That's around the time she and my father separated. On her own, my mother worked extra hard. She wasn't a great engineer, but she demonstrated exceptional managerial skills. She quickly climbed the ladder to Spen Fazer, and kept going all the way up to Sef Vobot Monogh."

"Impressive!"

"You don't have to tell me! The Frybar awarded her the Sune of Spen. Then they gave her this blue star."

His mouth full of vegetables, Jinto just nodded.

"So you see, I am genetically a lander. When I was your age, that made me furious—who wants to grow old and die, right?" The old man paused wistfully. "But when you get to be my age, you realize that you wouldn't even know what to do with an eternally young body anyway. Of course, you wouldn't understand that."

"No, probably not."

"The body and soul should grow old together." The old man chewed a piece of chicken. "To get back to the story, I was able to apply for enrollment in the Kenru because my mother was a Lef. Without Frokaj, I couldn't be a Lodair Norkuta, like a Lodair Gariar. Thus, I signed up for Kenru Fazel Har. You know what that is?"

"Yes, I also took *that* entrance exam. I don't have much interest in being a ship designer or engineer, though."

"Luckily, I got to be a Lodair Fazer Hal. When my mother got her Sune and Skor, my engineering skills really came in handy. Ultimately, that is the egg from which our plot hatches."

"What?" Jinto asked, thinking he missed something.

"The plan to get you out of here. Our plot to overturn my son? You didn't forget, did you?" the old man teased.

"Please! I haven't been able to think about anything else!"

"Even during my compelling story?" The Lyuf Raika seemed happy to bust Jinto's chops.

"Well, no, not exactly . . ." Jinto blushed.

The old man chuckled. "Don't sweat it. It's been a long time since I've had anyone to talk to. I know I tend to ramble."

"That's not true. It was all very . . . interesting."

"You know, Faneb, you seem like a decent guy, so you shouldn't lie, not even to humor an old man."

Jinto paled.

"Now, let's get back to the matter at hand. Ships and Garish have certain things in common. Essentially, a Garish is just a ship without an engine, right? Well, I designed this Lyumex. And I never handed the plans over to my son. That damn hothead locked me up before he was even officially in charge! What he doesn't know is that with a single Sejiyos, I can control this house's computer network. With the right password, I could use any terminal in the house to teach him a thing or two."

"Then why—"

"Why am I content to be a prisoner? Tell me this, boy: if I escaped, where would I go? A three Kelvin vacuum surrounds the Lyumex. All the Gosuk who were sympathetic to my plight got their walking papers a long time ago. There's no point in escaping."

"You could ask for help."

"The Frybar won't interfere in a nobleman's household affairs. Remember that, since you're noble, too. Anyway, I like this life. True, I am trapped here, but there's nowhere else I want to go. I don't want to see any of my old friends. I'm the only one who's aged, so it's weird."

" 'The body should age with the soul,' right?"

"Oh, you *were* listening to this old man's ramblings!"

Jinto smiled.

"Then I don't need to explain."

"Well, that all makes sense. But . . ." Even if he could believe the Lyuf Raika, there were still unknowns in the equation. "How do you know the Lyuf hasn't changed the Sejiyos?"

"I don't," the former baron stated frankly. "Sometimes you just have to gamble. If you don't take any chances, life is boring as hell. My biggest complaint here is that I have no one to gamble with."

"I hate gambling." Ever since his father's political gamble seven years before, Jinto had felt as though taking a chance on destiny was simply sinful.

"That's normal. But keep in mind that the odds on this bet are good. Really good. The Sejiyos is burned into the molecular structure—as long as he hasn't swapped out all the Datykirl, we're golden."

"Oh yeah?" With no evidence that the password would work, Jinto remained skeptical.

"You have to trust me, Faneb. Bet on me. Now, tell me about *your* problems. Why are you here?"

Jinto gladly (and quickly) recapped the story of his time on the *Gosroth*, their encounter with the enemy fleet, his escape with Lafiel in the Pelia, their mission to alert the Frybar, and their pit stop in Lyumusko Febdak for supplies. "And you know the rest, Lonyu Lyum Raika."

"So that girl you call Lafiel is actually Feia Lartneir?"

"Yes." Jinto nodded.

"Holy cow." The old man grinned. "Of course this had to happen *after* I grew old and retired. Amazing! My dear late mother would have been so pleased to receive Feia Lartneir. Even a mere count is a good guest, but this! Wow. Our family's stock just went up, I'd say."

"Please," Jinto pleaded, "will you help me?"

"Of course. How about I get you and Feia Lartneir aboard the Pelia and make it fly? That work for you?"

Jinto brightened. "Yes, but we'll need fuel."

"Right, right, can't forget the fuel. Oh. And food. Please take some food for your journey."

"That would be great. Just between you and me, Waniil gets old pretty fast."

"Great. There's just one problem."

"What's that?" Jinto asked.

"Well, I need to get to a Soteyua. That no-good son of mine doesn't trust me at all; there's no terminal in this confinement area."

"Oh no!" The wind came out of Jinto's sails.

"Did you really think it would be that easy? I'd just command the Soteyua, and you and your girlfriend could run off and get married and live happily ever after? The world isn't that sweet."

"She's not my girlfriend," Jinto pointed out.

"That's too bad. I heard she's a real cutie."

Jinto ignored this. "How can we get to a Soteyua?"

"Obviously we'll have to leave this gilded cage."

"Right, but how are we going to do that?"

"That is the question. We'll need to think of a plan that will make you look really good in front of your girlfriend."

"She's *not* my girlfriend." Jinto huffed.

"Are you sure?"

"Yes, I'm sure." However, even as he insisted, Jinto realized that he sort of wished she was.

"That's a shame. I was kind of hoping my son could be the third side of a sordid Imperial love triangle." He cackled.

Of course, there was nothing sordid about Lyuf Febdak's interactions with Lafiel.

In fact, there were (uncharacteristically) no sordid interactions at all that night; the Lyuf retired solo. Normally, a few of his favorite Gosuk accompanied him, but that night, he had a lot to ponder.

Sipping Rinmo from an amethyst wine glass (or Breskirl Lamteysh), the baron second-guessed the choices that he'd made that day.

Although he had a tendency to overestimate his intelligence, the baron was not crazy or stupid. He knew his Lyumusko could not stand up against the Frybar, but he regarded it as his own kingdom and trusted that he'd done the right thing to protect it.

Yes, in his own Skor, he could easily immerse himself in the illusion that he was the big banana, the leader of an independent kingdom.

When he'd intercepted the communication between Lafiel and Space Traffic Control, he'd immediately feared the worst—losing his private paradise.

Even from a remote Skor, the Lyuf had enough sense of the outside world to guess that the enemy was likely the Four Nations Alliance. All he could do now was cling to the thin hope that they would ignore the Lyumusko. For this to happen, he would have to stop anybody from passing through Sord Febdak.

Lafiel sure wasn't impressed with that explanation, he thought. The baron knew there was a low probability that the Skor would attract the enemy's attention by itself. At first he considered rushing the resupply job and sending the Pelia back on its way very quickly, hoping it might draw the enemy away from his Skor. But then he had a horrible thought. *What if the enemy is already aiming for the Lyumusko?*

In that case, all the Lyuf could do was submit. He had no military of any kind, so resistance would be futile. He would, however, be willing to give them as much antimatter fuel as they wanted if they would leave him alone.

But suppose the enemy didn't want or need his cooperation? There was a high probability they would just take the Joth (and everything else) by force.

In that case, it might come in handy to keep the grand-daughter of the Spunej as a bartering chip.

The Spunej wouldn't compromise any battles to save a hostage, even if it was her granddaughter, but the baron had to count on the enemy being ignorant of this fact.

With Lafiel, he could negotiate the preservation of his Ribeun. He would probably have to hand her over, maybe even make Lyumusko Febdak into a Four Nations Alliance army base. But he was confident that once it became an essential fuel base, the territory would regain its autonomy.

But what if I cut ties to the Frybar, and then the enemy never comes?

In that case, he would be the supreme ruler of his own little universe. So what if he only had fifty vassals, and so what if he would only ever taste a small fraction of universal cuisine?

He would be the king of his own perfect world.

The Lyuf thought about being the king with Lafiel as one of his subjects.

If he were to dissociate from the Frybar, her rank as Lartnei would cease to feed his inferiority complex because she would have no authority in his Skor. The Gosuk, all handpicked and obedient women, would continue to worship the baron like a god. This seemed like the best possible outcome.

Honestly, the baron rarely socialized with Abh women. Although he met many Abh women on Lakfakalle and in the military, they invariably made him nervous.

In order to address these fears, from time to time, he had one of the vassals dye her hair blue and dress up like Abh nobility. Sadly, a Gosuk dressed like an Abh was just that—outwardly pleasant, but somehow disappointing. Unlike real Abh women, the Gosuk were simply too modest.

Until he encountered Lafiel, he'd nearly forgotten what real Abh women were like.

The Lyuf grinned as he refilled his glass with more Rinmo.

He doubted that this encounter would have been as comfortable for him on Lakfakalle. His sense of ease was indisputably a result of having the homefield advantage. It was like a rehearsal for his reign to come.

Then the thought, *But a kingdom will need an heir*, leapt into his drunken mind. *There are plenty of women here, but they're all landers.*

Having a child with a lander would almost certainly result in a terminal hereditary defect unless the child was genetically modified. Of course, there were tons of medical facilities in the Frybar capable of that kind of genetic engineering. The baron himself came from one such baby factory.

However, there were no such facilities in Lyumusko Febdak.

Now, Lafiel was unquestionably Abh. Biologically, at least, there would be no problem creating an heir.

The only conceivable drawback was that natural conception was such a crapshoot; the numbers were in favor of a biological masterpiece, but genetic perfection was not guaranteed. The baron once read a report stating that at most one in fifty natural-born people would have a serious ailment. But that was less than two percent.

As gambles went, he liked those odds.

Yes . . . The Lartnei will bear my children.

His corrupt imagination ran amok. The Lyuf supposed he would be the first to make love to the Lartnei. Of course, he would have to wait; although she was quite beautiful, she was still much too young for him. He would have to wait a long time until she was a grown woman.

At any rate, he had gotten ahead of himself. The Frybar might still recover this territory. And just in case that happened, he had to continue to treat Lafiel with the utmost formality and civility.

Although he wasn't courteous to the young count, he hadn't abused the lander boy, either. Besides, how bad would it look that he left the count in the care of his father?

Now. The Pelia. That might be a problem. Maybe I should destroy it. But how could I ever explain that to the Frybar? No, better hold off on that until I know more about the situation.

If the Frybar decided not to return, then the Lyuf could do whatever he wanted. By that time, surely the Lartnei would come to see his better qualities.

I can even use that despicable lander, he thought, *to provide sperm samples for future generations of Gosuk.*

In a pleasant Skiade-induced fog, the Lyuf exhaled all his doubts and worries.

After chugging all the Rinmo in his cup, the baron flopped onto his bed. At that exact moment, the Luode rang.

"It better be important," the baron answered.

"This is Household Staff Greida here. Sorry to bother you while you're sleeping, Your Excellency, but there are intruders in the Pelia. What should I do?"

The baron leapt out of bed.

The baron overlooked one major thing; Abh good looks were not unique to him alone.

The Lyuf's handsome features were unusual on land worlds, so the Gosuk revered him. They cherished everything he gave them, whether it was a box of chocolates or a sound beating. Or if they didn't, he simply sent them packing.

What he didn't count on was the fact that the demigod good looks that entranced his Gosuk were common to all Kasarl Gereulak.

About half of the baron's Gosuk were loyal specifically to him. The remaining servants were merely fascinated by the entire Abh race. In reality, their love of all things Abh was so great that they were enraptured by a mere baron—a rank very common among Abh nobility. Seelnay was one such woman.

Whenever she got a chance, she snuck glances at holograms of Abh noblemen. Although she wasn't attracted to women, she was completely enamored of the Abh Lartnei from the moment she set eyes on Lafiel.

Living in a remote territory with the baron for so many years, she'd come to view it as a kind of paradise, and she was grateful to the baron for letting her live there so long. Over time, she came to view his orders as absolute.

That changed, however, when Lafiel came. The Lartnei's words echoed in Seelnay's ears and left a deep impression. *This girl might become the Spunej someday.*

As soon as Seelnay settled her internal battle, she felt greatly relieved. She was extremely happy to serve the Lartnei.

Without asking any more questions, she faithfully led the Lartnei to the Dobroria, then waited for her to return.

At last, Lafiel came back. Her robe appeared slightly bulky around the thighs.

"Feia Lartneir." Seelnay knelt.

"Gosuk Seelnay," Lafiel said, "please take me to Jinto. Or else, bring Jinto to me. Can you do that?"

"Jinto?" Seelnay had no idea who that was.

"My companion. Jarluk Dreu Haider. The prisoner. You've met him."

The girl sighed audibly. The name Jarluk Dreu conjured the image of a blue-haired nobleman, but Lafiel meant the lander boy masquerading as a noble. "That guy?"

"Yes. Do you know where he is?"

"No. I'm sorry."

"No need to apologize." Lafiel sounded irritated.

"You're too kind."

"Then do you know where the Lyuf Raika is? The other prisoner?"

"Master's father?" Seelnay asked disdainfully. "He's not a prisoner. He's retired."

"Imprisoned, retired, whatever. Jinto's probably with him, so we need to find the former baron somehow."

"I'm sorry," Seelnay cringed, "but that's impossible."

"Lyuf's orders?"

"There's that, but I couldn't even do it anyway."

"It's sealed?"

"Yes."

"Can you contact Lyuf Raika?"

"You could talk on the Luode in the household staff room, but only a few vassals are allowed to go in there."

"Are you one of those few?"

"Forget it. There are always other people in there. They won't let us."

Lafiel pulled a weapon out from under her robe. "Maybe we can convince them. Can you use this?" She offered it to Seelnay.

"No. I've never used one before." Seelnay couldn't believe the Lartnei would trust her with so much responsibility.

"It's easy." Lafiel pulled another gun out from the Kutaroev on her thigh and gave Seelnay a brief demonstration.

"Okay. I think I understand. Once the safety switch is off, I just aim the thing and pull the trigger."

"Good. Let's go." Lafiel took off running.

Seelnay ran after her.

There were a bunch of doors, so Seelnay had to lead the way. When they reached the last door, Seelnay panicked. *Is this treason?* She shuddered.

Earlier, she hadn't had time to think about the consequences. Taking a deep breath, Seelnay sent an ID code from her Kreuno, unlocking the door.

"O-open . . ." Seelnay's voice wavered. She turned around. "Feia Lartneir."

"What?" Lafiel said as she began to walk through the door.

Seelnay trotted after her. "I have the right to petition."

"Proceed."

"After this offense against my master, I can't stay in the Lyumusko. Please, Feia Lartneir, add me to the ranks of your Gosuk."

Stunned, Lafiel turned around.

Turning red, Seelnay feared she might have overstepped her boundaries.

"Yes, I'll gladly do that," said Lafiel, "although, you'll be the first."

"No way!" Seelnay couldn't believe a Fasanzoerl could exist without even one vassal.

"Of course, Lartei Kryb has plenty of Gosuk. And even though it's my father who's in charge of this kind of thing, I think that, given the circumstances, we'll manage to take you in somehow."

"When you say 'father,' do you mean Feia Larth Kryb?"

"Yes."

Again the sensation of being in close proximity to royalty struck Seelnay.

"However, your skills as an antimatter Baikok specialist will likely go to waste serving my family."

"I'm honored." Seelnay couldn't believe the Lartnei remembered her job! The urge to cry assaulted her, causing her eyes to well up with tears.

"Stop that," Lafiel said, disgusted.

"Stop what?" Seelnay asked seriously, afraid she'd offended Lafiel.

"Forget it. But don't you think you ought to go somewhere that won't waste your skills?"

"I'm so glad you care about the future of a lowly servant like me, but, Feia Lartneir, I can't stay here."

"Right." Lafiel nodded. "Let's get out of here, but afterward, I can't promise you that you will work for the Lartei."

"Your good intention is enough." At least Lafiel would take her as far as Bar Nirort.

They came to another door, very close now to the household rooms.

Anticipating great adventures to come, Seelnay opened the door.

Though it was merely a footnote in Lafiel's life, what happened next would become a seminal incident in Lyumusko Febdak's short history.

To be continued in
Seikai: Crest of the Stars: A Modest War

Appendix:
Imperial Star Force Officer Ranks

Imperially-appointed Officers

Flight (Garia):

Kilo-Commander (Shewas)

Associate Admiral (Roifrode)

Admiral (Frode)

Grand Admiral (Fofrode)

Star Force Field Marshal (Spen Laburar)

Imperial Field Marshal (Rue Spen)

Administration (Sazoir):

Administrative Kilo-Commander (Shewas Sazoirl)

Administrative Associate Admiral (Roifrode Sazoirl)

Administrative Admiral (Frode Sazoirl)

Administrative Grand Admiral (Fofrode Sazoirl)

Administrative Field Marshal (Spen Sazoirl)

Emperor-appointed Officers

Flight (Garia)

Line Wing Pilot (Fektodai)

Rear Guard Pilot (Rinjer)

Forward Duty Pilot (Lekle)

Deca-Commander (Lowas)

Deputy Hecto-Commander (Roibomowas)

Hecto-Commander (Bomowas)

Administration (Sazoir)

Administrative Line Wing Officer (Fektodai Sazoirl)

Administrative Rear Guard Officer (Rinjer Sazoirl)

Administrative Forward Duty Officer (Lekle Sazoirl)

Administrative Deca-Commander (Lowas Sazoirl)

Administrative Deputy Hecto-Commander
(Roibomowas Sazoirl)

Administrative Hecto-Commander (Bomowas Sazoirl)

At this time, the Abh primarily use big ships with big guns, but at the founding of the Empire, they relied on more agile battle units that held up to only three people. The control and command officers of those units were flight officers.

The Star Force utilized four-ship formations. The commander flew at the nose of the diamond shape, and the junior commander took the tail. Hence, the commander was known as Advance Guard Flight Officer, and the junior commander was Rear Guard Flight Officer. The pilots on the left and right sides were called Line Wing Flight Officers. In certain battles, it would be necessary for the formation to split up. In these instances, the Advance Guard and Rear Guard Flight Officers each led one Line Wing Flight Officer. Sometimes, two of these diamond formations joined forces to create an even more impressive battle unit. The commander ships were each accompanied by an automated drone, so there were ten total ships in the group, and the highest ranking officer was sensibly called Deca-Commander.

In the days when all the Abh lived aboard their city-ship, the *Abriel*, they had somewhere between one hundred and two hundred ships in their fleet. Although the exact number was uncertain, they called the commander-in-chief of the battle unit Hecto-Commander. There were a few Vice-Hecto-Commanders on hand to assist him.

As the Star Force grew in size and numbers, it became apparent that they needed to create a higher rank for the top battle officer. The next step up the ladder became Kilo-Commander, even though the system of ranking based strictly on machine numbers had already become inexact and nebulous.

After the founding of the Frybar, the Abh started using multiple motherships. When the need arose to name the leader of a group of motherships, they chose Admiral.

As the number of motherships increased, the Admirals needed to delegate authority to someone who could lead partial fleets. These people were Associate Admirals.

Ultimately, the Abh decided it was better to use larger vessels instead of their high-mobility units, so the titles up to Hecto-Commander became obsolete.

But the expansion of the Empire continued, and the Star Force increased proportionally.

When multiple fleets became standard, they needed to make a rank higher than Admiral. They settled on Grand Admiral and Field Marshal.

New ranks arose when the Abh discovered the need to engage in land battles. It was entirely necessary to establish and maintain control over some unruly planets.

Thus, they created a Land Force. Field Marshals were then split into Star Force Field Marshals and Land Force Field Marshals. Imperial Field Marshals outranked them both.

The period in which the Labule had two armies didn't last long. Flight Officers (and up), even though they were landers, were Lef and nobles, which meant they were regarded as Abh. They weren't satisfied, however, and sought the abolition of Imperial rule. Their insurrection, dubbed The Jhimryua Revolt after its ringleader, was the largest in Imperial history.

After this uprising, which was a big black eye for the Empire, the Frybar decided to dismantle the Land Force, which was comprised primarily of landers, anyway. From that point on, the land battle units became part of the airborne department; they weren't a separate army, but they were stationed in local governments and fleets.

So the Land Force Field Marshals became Airborne Field Marshals. As the local departments grew, new ranks popped up, like Administrative Field Marshal, Military

Physician Field Marshal, Engineer Field Marshal, and so forth.

As far as specialty departments go, there are: the airborne department, military physician department, engineering department (for all of which the highest rank is Field Marshal); the guard department, judicial affairs department, nursing department (for these three, the highest rank is Grand Admiral); the military mechanics department, arms department, shipbuilding department, machine building department, photonics department, routes department (for the above, the highest rank is Admiral; higher ranks integrate into the engineering department); and the military music department (highest rank is Hecto-Commander).

Notes from the Editor and Fan Consultants:

As Morioka-sensei has stated no rules for upper or lower case Barohn, please note that all Abh words in Romanized form are capitalized.

All silent letters are removed. In most cases, vowels are pronounced as they would be in Italian.

Changes to the endings of certain nouns (pertaining to direction, possession, etc.) are due to the Baronh noun declension system. Example: The nominative Lodairl becomes Lodair when used in the possessive.

The letter **C** always makes a hard consonant sound, so **C** becomes **K** in this text.

There is no **J** in authentic Baronh, but for phonetic purposes, an **Ï** becomes **J**, and the soft 'ge' sound (like in 'page') is spelled 'jhe' (as in 'Ruejhe').

Unlike Japanese, Baronh has a clear distinction between the letters **R** and **L**. A semi-rolled **R** is spelled "rl" here.

There is no **W** in authentic Baronh, but for phonetic purposes, an **Ü** becomes **W**.

The letter **Y** is never used as a vowel or given its own individual syllabic emphasis.

In written Barohn, there's a distinction between a voiced "th" and an unvoiced "th." For the sake of simplicity, we did not make the distinction in written Baronh here.

For more information, do a web search for "Baronh" and visit fan sites like the following:

For pronunciation rules:
http://www.geocities.com/gatewaytoseikai/1_en.html

For characters' names, military ranks, culture, history, etc.:
http://www.geocities.com/Tokyo/Shrine/4777/Seikai/seikai.html

A Baronh-Japanese Only Dictionary:
http://dadh-baronr.s5.xrea.com/doc/baronhdic-1.html#A

For a comprehensive overview of the *Seikai* universe:
http://www.abhnation.com/

If you read Japanese, try the two Reader Guides entitled *Seikai no Monshou Dokuhon* (1999) and *Seikai no Senki Dokuhon* (2001).

Glossary

A

Aga Izomia	Challenge to battle
Aibs	Lander
Aith	Country, nation
Ajh	Crest, coat of arms
Alek	Battle-line ship
Alm Drokia	Senior Communications Officer
Alm Kasarlia	Executive Officer
Alm Rilbiga	Senior Navigator (similar to Alm Lodair)
Alm Tlakia	Senior Gunnery Officer
Alpha	Abh control tiara
Alpha Klabrar	An tiara with a wing on one side
Alpha Matbrar	A tiara with two wings
Apezm	Sash clip
Apyuf	Seat belt
Arnej	Orbital tower
Arosh	The Imperial capital (Lakfakalle)

B

Baikok	Antimatter fuel tank
Baish	Antimatter fuel
Bar Abh Lepenu	Pride of the Abh
Bar Nirort	Abh capitol
Bar Sif	Abh nobility
Banzorl Ludorlt	Recruitment Office
Banzorl Garyuk	Household rooms
Basev	Agricultural lands
Batia	Waiter or waitress
Bauria	Connecting ferry ship
Belyse	(Space Traffic) Control
Belysega	Controller
Bene Lodair	Pilot trainee, officer-in-training
Bes	Pier or dock

Besega	Moral educator
Bidaut	Spaceport
Bisiaf	Dining hall
Bitsairl	Subject
Bomowas	Hecto-Commander (Fleet Commander)
Bondev Sashu	Soldier working with hand weapons
Bore Rue Labule	Imperial Star Force-controlled area
Borl Paryun	Viscount(ess) of Paryun
Borsh	Control buttons
Borskor Paryun	Viscount(ess) Paryun's territory
Bosnal	Soldier
Breskirl	Amethyst
Bruvoth Gos Suyun	Four Nations Alliance
Busespas	Captain's badge
Bynkerl	Supervisor, Controller
Byr	Fleet
Byr Drok Lonid	Communications Fleet's base
Byr Kureyal	Training Fleet
Byr Ragrlot	Scout Fleet

C

D

Dadjocs	Normal space
Daemon	Standard gravity
Dagbosh	Self-rolling suitcase
Daisielle	Lift anchor
Darmesath Voflir	Imperial court rank (similar to Sune)
Dath	Normal space
Datykirl	Computer crystal
Daush	Long robe
Defath	Electromagnetic family crest; ID information
Delktou	Delktou Space Station
Derlash	Elements of heredity
Dersluf Bos	Trout wrapped in sticky rice balls
Dobroria	Ascent-descent tube
Dores	Tray
Dreu	Count(ess)

Dreu Gemufadofia Lamryunar	Her Majesty Lamryuna, Countess of Gemufarth
Dreu Haider	Count Hyde
Dreuhynu Friizal	Count Friiza's nation
Dreuhynu Haider	Count Hyde's nation
Dreuhynu Vorlak	Count Vorash's nation
Dreujhe	Count's family
Dreujhe Vorlak	Count Vorash's family
Driaron	Big Bang
Drokia	Communications Officer
Drokia Roirosasel	Investigation and Communications Officer
Drosh Flacteder	Inter-space-time bubble communication
Duhyu	Bath towel
Duniit	Alarm bell

E

Eifu	Computer network

F

Fal Feia Kufena	My Lovely Highness
Fal Sif	My lord, my master
Faneb	Young man
Faniiga	The former emperors
Fapyut	Sovereign
Fasanzoerl	Imperial family
Fath	Plane Space
Fathoth	Plane Space navigation
Faz Fathoth	Plane Space navigation technology
Fazuia Robon	Weapons Department
Feia	His / Her / Your Highness
Feia Lartneir	Her Highness the Queen
Feia Ruer	Her Highness the Imperial Princess
Fektodai	Aviator
Feretocork	Ascent-descent platform
Feroth	Abh maturity, after about age fifteen
Fiith	Family name
Flasath	Time-space bubble
Flasatia	Time-space bubble creation engine

Flirish	Imperial or Royal Court
Flisesia	Antiannihilation engine
Frash	Round-trip ship
Frokaj	Alpha spatial recall device used to "feel" space
Frosh	Space-sense organ in an Abh's forehead
Fruk Saran	Mother's son
Frybar	Empire (n.) or Imperial (adj.)
Frybar Gloer Gor Bari	Humankind Empire of Abh
Fryum Loran	Father's daughter
Fryum Neg	Daughter of love
Futaria Bosnal	Military registration number
Futaria Surofwot	Duty number

G

Ga Lartei	Eight Royal Houses
Gahorl	Ship's bridge
Gairit	Military doctor
Gal Skas	Imperial crest medal
Garia Lodair	Flight Officer
Garish	Orbital residence
Glaharerl Rue Byrer	Imperial Fleet Commander-in-Chief
Glaik	Hydroponic farm
Gloe	Humans
Gooheik	Control glove
Gor Lyutcoth	Separate space-time bubbles
Gor Putarloth	Space-time fusion
Goriaav	Landing / departure deck
Gorv	Bathroom
Gosnoh	No abnormalities; everything A-OK
Gosuk	Vassal(s)
Gosuk Ran	Honorable Vassal
Gosuk Lyum	Baron's vassal(s)
Grei	Chopsticks
Greu	Command stick or cane
Guraw Mongarl	Ship's banner
Gusath	Bathrobe
Guzas	Shower
Gryhynu	Nation of Lilies

H

Hoksath	Mine(s)
Hoksatjocs	Mine battles
Horl	Hold, hatch

I

Irgyuf	Electromagnetic projection cannon
Isath	Supply vessel

J

Ja Fe, Ja Flasath	Map of Plane Space
Jadbyr	Partial fleet / squadron
Janarlmukos	Genetic inspection
Japer	Light source magazines (ammo for Klanyu)
Janyu	Artificial womb
Jazria	Mobile pedestal
Jhedirl	Family traditions
Joth	Antimatter fuel factory

K

Kaimukoth	Acceleration
Kalique	Shuttle (smaller than a Pelia or Longia)
Kasarl Gereulak	"Kin of the Stars" (the Abh)
Kasorvia Bender	Hydrogen transport ship
Kedlairl	Imperial nautical mile
Kenyu	Trainee
Kenru	Military Academy
Kenru Faziar Har	Shipbuilding School
Kenru Faziar Robon	Weapons School
Kenru Sazoir	Administration School
Kesateudo	Residents of space
Kesath	Space, the universe
Kiigaf	Volcanoes
Kilugraj	Inheritance of the Imperial throne
Kilugia	Crown Prince / Princess
Kiseg	Connection chains
Klanraj	Lasers, laser beams

Klanyu	Laser pistols
Klejaga	Training ships
Kloferl Fathot	Plane Space navigation theory
Kos Kisegal	Function crystal
Kreuno	Abh communication wrist device
Kuro	Control desk
Kutaroev	Decorative sash
Kyua Plakia	Lady Plakia (Lexshu)

L

Labule	Star Force
Lamteysh	Wine glasses
Larliin	Gene sponsor; provider of genes
Larosh	Highest-ranking Officer
Lartbei	Royal Palace
Lartei	Royal family
Lartei Balgzeder	Royal House of Balgzede
Lartei Barker	Royal House of Barke
Lartei Irik	Royal House of Iriish
Lartei Kryb	Royal House of Kryv
Lartei Lasiser	Royal House of Lasis
Lartei Shulgzeder	Royal House of Shulgzede
Lartei Skirh	Royal House of Skirl
Lartei Weskor	Royal House of Wesko
Larth	King or Queen
Larth Kryb Feia Debeus	His Majesty King of Kryv
Lartnei	Queen
Lartnei Kasna	First Queen
Lartraj	Throne
Latonyu	Battle command console
Lef	Landed family, the "gentry"
Lekle	Vanguard Flight Officer
Lenyj	Antiproton cannon
Lesliamroth	Emergency
Lo	Ship's hatch
Lodairl	Officer
Lodairl Fazel Hal	Shipbuilding Officer
Lodairl Gariar	Flight Officer

Lodairl Norkuta	Regular Officer
Lodairl Sazoir	Administrative Officer
Loebehynu Sufagnaum	Marquis Safugnoff's star system
Lonid	Base
Lonjhoth Rirrag	Data concatenation
Lonyu	Your / His / Her Excellency
Lonyu Lyum	Your / His Excellency the Baron
Lonyu Jarluker Dreur	Your / His Excellency the Count's Son
Lowas	Deca-Commander
Lowas Sazoir	Administrative Deca-Commander
Lowas Skem	Engineering Deca-Commander
Luode	A telephone-like device
Luse	Second-in-Command
Luzei Fanigalak	Former Emperors' Congress
Lyuel Kunasot Kenrur Sazoir	Administrative students' rulse
Lyuf	Baron
Lyuf Raika	Former Baron
Lyumex Febdak	Baron Febdash's mansion
Lyumjhe Febdak	Baron Febdash's family
Lyumjhe	Baron's family
Lyumusko Febdak	Baron Febdash's territory

M

Mei	Pipe, whistle
Menraj	Plane Space navigation capability
Menyu	Spaceship(s) (especially Plane Space ships)
Menyu Sorna	Lightweight craft

N

Nahen	Land world(s)
Nigla	National badge
Nisoth	Your Grace
Noktaf	State of movement (within Fath)
Nui Abliarsar	The Abriel ears

O

Onhokia	Automatic mechanism
Onwarele	Mechanical teacher

Onyu	Idiot
Opsei	Main engines
Orton Fimferma	Sea turtle flippers

P

Parhynu	Country of Roses
Patmsaihoth	Welcome-aboard ceremony
Pelia	Coordination vessel, contact vessel
Ponowas	Ship command, ship supervision
Ponyu	Transport vessel
Putorahedesorf	Commander medal

Q

R

Rawarf	Clothesbasket
Rebisath	Passenger ship
Renyu	Rank
Resii	Patrol ship
Ribeun	Territories held by a Voda
Ribwasia	Paralysis gun
Rilbido	Navigation field
Rinjer	Rear Defense Officer
Rinmo	Hard apple cider
Riopos	Smoked thigh
Riwerl	Regulations
Rop	Abh fruit (like a lemon)
Rozgia	Carafe
Rue Bogne	Imperial grandchild
Rue Lalasa	Records of distinguished Imperial persons
Rue Lef	Imperial citizen
Rue Razem	Imperial law and domain
Rue Nigla	Imperial medal
Rue Spen	Imperial Admiral
Rue Sif	Imperial noble
Ruecoth	Imperial calendar year
Ruejhe	Imperial family, Imperial house
Ruene	Imperial Princess

Ryabon	Crystal ceramic

S

Saij Daifat Heita	Electromagnetic wave family crest key
Saparga	Commence battle
Saput	Pressurized spacesuit helmet
Sarerl / Sarerraj	Ship's Captain (similar to Shewas)
Sash	Crew member
Sash Gorna	Fourth-class crew member
Sash Leitofec	Guard
Sates Gor Hoksat	Maneuverable space-time mines
Satyrl	Liquid soap
Sazoirl	Administrator
Sedia	Pilot
Sedraleia	Imperially appointed pilot
Sef Vobot Monogh	Chief of Warship Administrative HQ
Sejiyos	Password
Serlin	Uniform
Sesuwas	Mass waves
Shirsh Guzar	Shower room
Shirsh Sediar	Cockpit
Shewas	Kilo-Commander (similar to Naval Captain)
Sif	Noble
Skalish	Old-fashioned serving table
Skas Lazasot	Imperial peers' legal system
Skemsoraj	Royal throne
Skemsorl	Imperial throne
Skemsorl Roen	Jade Imperial throne
Skiade	Alcohol
Skobrotaf	Stopped state (within Fath)
Skoem	Military Engineer
Skor	Territory
Skurleteria	Founding Emperor
Slymekoth	Military service
Slymekotraj	Duty
Sneseb	Defensive magnetic field
Sord	Gate in or out of Plane Space
Sord Febdak	Febdash Sord

Sord Gulark	Open Sord
Sord Kikotosokunbina Keik	Keish Sord 193
Sord Loeza	Closed Sord
Sord Sufagnaum	Safugnoff Sord
Sord Vorlak	Vorash Sord
Sorf	Bodysuit, pantsuit
Souk	Sailors, mariners
Sos	Territorial citizens, people
Soteyua	Computer terminal
Sov Vekekar	Fuel tank asteroid
Soyuth	Ship lock or gate
Spen	Fleet Admiral
Spen Fazer	Engineer of Admiral rank
Speshynu	Nation of Camellias
Spunej	Emperor, Empress
Spunej Ramaj Erumita	Her Majesty Empress Ramaj
Spyut	Nuclear fusion shells
Sune	Court rank or title
Supflasath	Space-time particles
Surgu	Coffee

T

Teal Nom	Peach juice
Tlakia Hoksak	Mine Gunnery Officer
Toserl	Representative, magistrate
Traiga	Title
Tyl Lashuban	Mandarin orange juice

U

V

Voda	Landed nobility
Voklanyu	Laser cannons
Voskura	Military University
Voskura Duner	Star Force Military University

W

Wameria	Gravity control mechanism

Postscript

Hi, I'm Hiroyuki Morioka. Most of you probably don't know me.

Although I am most experienced at writing simple sci-fi stories set in the not-so-distant future, for my debut (and I hope to write a lot more!) full-length work, I wanted to do something spectacular set in outer space.

My roots are in space sci-fi, which is heavily intertwined with heroic fantasy.

Once I became a sci-fi writer, I wanted to build, at least on paper, a great intergalactic Empire.

If I had to guess why I chose this as the subject for my first long work, I would say it was to surprise attack the people who were familiar with my short stories.

This project was very precious to me, and it was my intention to commence writing only after setting up a perfect world and plot through meticulous planning.

However, when I began planning the book, I just couldn't wait to start writing. I shoved a blank floppy disk into my computer and began hammering at the keys.

I had to amend and revise the setup later. Throughout the whole writing process, I kept a memo pad next to my word processor, on which I created the setup concurrently with the manuscript.

As far as the story goes, it was a situation where each twist and turn came as a surprise to *me!*

Despite this unorthodox method, I somehow finished *Crest of the Stars*. Including my days of amateur writing, it's my first *real* long work.

"The characters act as they please," people told me. I had no idea how to take that. Naturally, because I didn't write according to a plan, this meant it took a long time to go from tentative completion to publication.

The reason it took so long is that Hayakawa Library JA placed a lot of stock in squeezing the release numbers. This means that when a newcomer produced a novel that didn't finish in just one volume, timing was the most important factor in publication.

In hindsight, this process really helped me mature. Thanks to numerous rewrites, I think I was able to attain a higher degree of perfection.

And so, I've completed all the volumes.

I hope you enjoy this fantasy world almost as much as I hope to make shameless sci-fi fans groan. Well, I'll see you again, in the Postscript of *Crest of the Stars 2: A Modest War*.

—March 10, 1996